HOW TO ENJOY ANTIQUES

Here is a delightful introduction to the fascinating world of antiques which not only tells how to recognize and enjoy them, but explains the role of these decorative and useful objects in the history of the United States.

What makes this book particularly helpful for the inexperienced collector is that it covers, for the first time in one volume, all American antiques from 1600 to 1900 including those produced here as well as those imported from abroad. In its informative pages, you will learn about furniture, silver, pottery and porcelain, glass, pewter, tin, brass, copper, iron, fireplace and lighting equipment, pictures, and homemade textiles, as well as such lesser-known American antiques as prints, quilts and coverlets, minor metal wares, silhouettes, weathervanes, and even needlework.

Illustrating the simple, readable text are over three hundred charming drawings by Pauline W. Inman. They point out the identifying characteristics of specific antique types and also show how styles and designs changed from one period to another.

Alice Winchester is the editor of ANTIQUES Magazine, and the author of many articles and books on the subject. Whether you wish to use this book as a guide to evaluating your family treasures, a help in furnishing your home and in purchasing gifts, or as a refreshing sidelight on American history, you will also gain from it unusual insight into the opportunities, aspirations, and changing attitudes of three hundred years of American life.

"Particularly helpful to the inexperienced collector."—
New York Times.

HOW TO KNOW
American Antiques

by Alice Winchester

Illustrated by
Pauline W. Inman

A SIGNET BOOK from
NEW AMERICAN LIBRARY
TIMES MIRROR

SIGNET, SIGNET CLASSICS, MENTOR, PLUME AND MERIDIAN BOOKS
are published by The New American Library, Inc.,
1301 Avenue of the Americas, New York, New York 10019

19 20 21 22 23 24 25 26

PRINTED IN THE UNITED STATES OF AMERICA

CONTENTS

Identification of Antiques on Front Cover

1. How Old Is Antique?

To anyone who browses in the antique shops these days, the question "How old is antique?" seems to have many answers. Side by side with ancient-looking furniture and old-fashioned china we may find ruffled pink glass, buttons, and souvenir spoons, that are no older than ourselves. It is a bewildering array.

In 1930 the United States Government ruled that objects had to be at least a hundred years old to be classed as antiques, and so admitted duty free to this country. Since then antiques have often been defined as objects made before 1830.

In Europe, things as recent as that seem quite young. In contrast with classic temples or medieval cathedrals, a chair of 1700 is modern. No wonder Europeans sometimes smile indulgently when we speak of American antiques. Except for Indian relics and a few Spanish buildings in the Southwest, the oldest of them can boast barely three hundred years.

Yet we have the same contrast right here. To a New Englander who knows the pine furniture of Pilgrim days, or a Virginian familiar with the colonial plantation houses, a Victorian sofa does not seem antique. In Indiana or Nebraska or Oregon it does, because it represents the earliest homes in the region. The age of antiques seems to vary in relation to their environment.

We have adopted as American antiques all sorts of things made and used here since the days of settlement. Brought from many lands, hewn out of the forests of the wilderness, carried across the mountains to new frontiers, they range from expedients to embellishments. From the functional pine chests of the Pilgrims to the last carved rose of the Victorians, they are the things America has grown up with and loved.

We enjoy living with them still, partly because we find them satisfying artistically, and partly because they are a link with our own past.

We often count among our antiques things made by machine as well as those wrought by hand. Most of these are later than 1830. That date does, however, serve as a dividing line between the age of craftsmanship and the machine age.

The transition did not occur overnight, of course. It had begun before 1800, and continued with gradual industrialization of the old-time crafts. By 1830 new methods of manufacturing, transportation, and communication affected the things people used in their houses, the way they lived, the very way they thought. We have to look at the machine-made objects of 1830 to 1900 differently from the handmade products of craftsmanship, but we can see in them just as clear an expression of the tastes and habits of the people who made and used them.

Legends grow on antiques the way moss grows on trees. As a family heirloom is passed from one generation to the next, its history takes on added flourishes. A spinning wheel made in 1820 becomes the spinning wheel brought over on the Mayflower. A bed of 1840 becomes the bed George Washington slept in.

But while the personal associations of our heirlooms add to their interest, we do not need to rely on traditions to place their date and source. Not every old piece has a pedigree, or a maker's mark or label, but every one has characteristics that identify it. The secret of where and when and by whom it was made is written in its material, its design, and its workmanship. And the facts about antiques are so much more fascinating than the legends that there is no need to embellish them.

2. *Furniture*

The name "early American furniture" means different things to different people. To many it means simple, rather crude tables and cupboards in pine and maple, with a Boston rocker and a Hitchcock or windsor chair thrown in. Or it means the horsehair sofas and marble-topped tables our grandmothers had in their parlors. To specialized collectors it may mean the Hadley chests and Carver chairs made here in the days of the Pilgrims. To others it will mean all the furniture made in America before about 1830 when machine-made pieces had begun to appear. *Early* has come to be as elastic as *antique*.

So to get a complete picture of our old furniture, we have to look at all the different kinds, very early and not so early, and there are a good many of them. Contrary to popular belief, the crude pine and maple is only a small part of it.

It is a great mistake to assume that any really fine pieces used here must have come from abroad. If you want to see how elegant we could be, look at the highboy pictured on page 42, and the chairs on page 33. There was of course a great deal of furniture made in our native woods, but American cabinetmakers also knew how to handle mahogany and satinwood with great skill and to ornament them with carving, inlay, and gilding.

Incidentally, the native woods they used were not all pine and maple, by any means. We should remember that they included walnut and cherry, oak, poplar, butternut and fruitwoods, hickory and ash, among others.

As the first step in getting the whole picture of early American furniture, let us take the name in its popular sense of informal, "country" furniture in light-colored native woods, and see what we have in that group.

Country Furniture

In the first place, most of the unpretentious furniture that typifies this kind of "early American" was made after 1800, even after 1825. Of what was made in the 1600's, very little survives, and most of it is in museums. That of the 1700's is also rare now, not so rare as the earlier but scarce enough to be sought by museums and collectors, bought at substantial prices, and duly treasured.

This "pine and maple" of the 1800's is indeed country furniture, or kitchen furniture as it is also called. Much of it was homemade in country and frontier regions. Some of it tried to emulate the design and decoration of more elegant pieces of the time—and occasionally failed rather miserably, or succeeded in achieving a simplified version with real originality. A drop-leaf table, for instance, with a few round turnings on the square legs, may be quite awkward; while some painted chairs and carved cupboards have a charming naiveté. Often the most successful pieces are those that were made from necessity, for purely utilitarian purposes and with no attempt at elaboration.

Besides simple chairs and tables, chests and cupboards, people have lately discovered various old pieces like lazy susans, milk or pie safes, cobbler's benches, and so-called dry sinks and water benches. They call these early American, though it is doubtful whether many of them are over a hundred years old.

The sinks and benches are lowly pieces that used to stand in the country kitchen

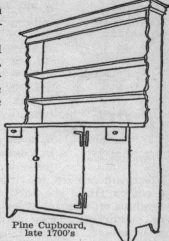

Pine Cupboard,
late 1700's

or back entry to hold a washbowel and pitcher. The lazy susan, found especially in the South and Midwest, is a revolving stand usually fixed in the center of a round dining table.

Milk or pie safes, also found in the Midwest and in Pennsylvania, took the place of refrigerators. They are simple cupboards whose doors have tin panels pierced in a decorative pattern to let air circulate through them.

Slat-Back Chair

Some of these do date from the 1820's or so, but such things continued to be used until after the Civil War. The cobbler's bench, which has been frequently reproduced and is often used as a coffee table, is a sore subject with many collectors of antiques, who see in it no artistic merit to start with, and find it utterly unsuitable as a piece of living-room furniture.

Two types of chairs made through the 1800's and even to this very day first appeared in the early 1700's and have shown only minor variations since: the *slat-back* and the *windsor*.

New England
Windsor Chair

Early slat-backs have turned legs, posts, and stretchers, and slats gracefully curved both up for looks and back for comfort, sometimes as many as seven in number.

Later ones became simpler, the slats fewer, the turnings less pronounced, and nineteenth-century examples are quite plain. Seats are normally rush.

Windsor chairs are believed to have originated near Windsor Castle in England, but the American examples are quite different from English, which are heavier and usually have a wide splat in the back. American windsors are of many types, identified by descriptive names: bow-back or loop-back, comb-back, fan-back, hoop-back, low-back, writing-arm. New England examples are usually more delicate than those made elsewhere. Pennsylvania examples often have ball feet.

Quality in a windsor depends on shaping of seat, boldness of rake of legs, vigor of turnings, soundness of construction, and general balance of proportions. Those of the 1700's are

Pennsylvania
Windsor Chair

usually better in all these respects. After 1790, especially, windsors were made with "bamboo" turnings, the legs, stretchers, and spindles shaped and ridged like sticks of bamboo.

Numerous small inexpensive chairs of the 1820's and later, often with a wide top rail and arrow-shaped spindles in the back, are really windsors. The essential character of the windsor is its "stick" construction: the outer sides of the back, like the spindles, are stuck into the seat instead of being a

Hitchcock Chair

continuation of the back legs; the legs too are stuck into the seat instead of being joined to it in a seat frame. Windsor settees, with the same construction, range in length from two-seaters to eight-legged pieces as much as seven feet long. Windsors were made of a combination of woods, for strength, and were usually painted.

In the 1820's the *Hitchcock chair* appeared, first produced by Lambert Hitchcock at Hitchcocksville, Connecticut. Unassuming and inexpensive as it was, it marked a milestone in furniture history because it was our first mass-produced piece of furniture. The chairs were made, assembled, and decorated by factory methods and shipped to all parts of the country.

Now Hitchcock's name is casually applied to any small, light, stenciled or painted chair, wherever produced. The ones he made, however, have his name stenciled along the back of the seat. The type was made through the 1840's, and is reproduced today.

Boston Rocker

The *Boston rocker* is related to the Hitchcock through its stenciled or painted decoration, and is about contemporary with it. Presumably the type originated in Boston, but it was made elsewhere too. The indefatigable Ben Franklin is credited with first putting rockers on a chair, and whether he deserves the credit or not, the invention was probably an American one. There are many derogatory comments about this infamous device in the writings of British visitors to America in the 1800's. Rockers have sometimes been added to old chairs, but the earliest rocking chairs, made as such, date from the late 1700's. They were slat-back. The Boston rocker with its slouchy lines and comfortable curves was the first rocking chair developed as an independent type.

About 1850 another mass-produced style became popular— *spool furniture*. Beds, chairs, washstands, tables, and some

Spool-Turned Table, 1850

Washstand, 1850

other forms had members turned to look like a string of spools or button molds. The beds especially are often favored today since with their low headboards and small proportions they are more manageable than high-post beds, and still they have a certain antiquity. They are

often called "Jenny Lind beds" because the type came in about the time the popular singer was touring the country for P. T. Barnum in 1850-1852. Spool furniture, like Hitchcock chairs, was inexpensive in its day.

It was, in fact, in response to the great demand for inexpensive furniture that furniture-making developed as an industry in the 1800's, fostered by the perfection of machines that made mass production pos-

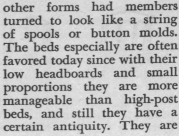

Bureau, 1850

sible. The shift from individual craftsmanship to machine methods began with Hitchcock and his chairs. Soon factories were established in the Middle West as well as in New England, and by the mid-century Grand Rapids had launched on its career as the leading furniture-making center in the country. Its products, made in local woods, were chiefly simplified and less costly versions of the

Bureau, 1850

Chairs of 1860-1870

fashionable styles of the time, and much of its painted "cottage furniture" of the 1860's to 1880's is what goes by the name of early American now.

Colonial Pine Furniture

Though most of the pine furniture you will find today is of the 1800's, what was made earlier is really a more important part of our picture. Our country furniture tradition was established in the first century of settlement in America, when the pine growing plentifully in local forests was used more than any other wood.

In those days cabinetmaking had not become a fully developed craft, and up to 1725 *turnery* and *joinery* were the important processes in furniture-making. Turning a straight leg, arm, or stretcher on a lathe gave it an ornamental contour of ring, spool, and vase shapes. Joining them meant fastening the separate members firmly together with wooden joints such as *mortise and tenon*.

Chests, and other "case pieces," were usually composed of flat panels which were joined or *rabbeted* to upright pieces called *stiles* and horizontal ones called *rails*.

There was not much furniture in a colonial home at that time, and nowhere near the variety of pieces that we know now. Chairs and stools, tables, chests, cupboards, and beds were about all.

Turned and joined stools, called *joint stools,* were more

Butterfly Table, 1700

common than chairs. Tables were made similarly; they are called *turned, stretcher,* or *tavern tables.* Drop leaves were added to give a larger surface and were sometimes supported by extra legs with stretchers called *gatelegs.* The kind with a wide flat support shaped like a butterfly's wing, called *butterfly tables,* developed in the very late 1600's.

About the simplest kind of table, which was used from those early days and on through the 1700's, was the *trestle* or *sawbuck table.* It was really just a big board supported on a two-legged standard or an X-shaped trestle. The *hutch table* was a combination table and chest and even a chair as well: a flat board held in place by dowels could be lowered as the table top or raised to be the chair back, and the seat was the lid of a box.

Trestle Table, early 1700's

Banister-Back Chair, early 1700's

Some of the earliest chairs, *Brewster* and *Carver chairs,* had posts and legs, spindles in the back, arms, and stretchers, all turned. Late in the 1600's somewhat lighter types of *turned chair* developed which were made up to about 1725. Some had the back and seat caned. Some had rush seats and *banister backs*—a row of thin turned spindles or flat spokes. They usually had a shaped piece at the top called a *cresting.* Feet on these pieces were most commonly round turnings, but carved *Spanish feet* were more decorative.

Our earliest chests were plain five-board or paneled boxes with a flat lid. A distinctive type of the late 1600's and early 1700's is the *Hadley chest* of the Connecticut Valley, which has flat carving in large floral designs covering the front. Some other New England chests of the early period have turned *spindles,* or knobs of wood called *bosses,* applied for decoration. So do some of the larger, more elaborate pieces called *court cupboards,* which are also carved. Pennsylvania chests, which were made from the early 1700's on, are large and low, with or without a drawer or two, and often have painted decoration.

Gradually, higher and narrower chests were built, and more drawers were added at the bottom. Such pieces, with drawers but with a lidded section at the top, are called *blanket chests.*

By the early 1700's, when real cabinetmaking had developed, the chest had completed its evolution from a plain lidded box to the case

Blanket Chest, early 1700's

of drawers. The blanket chest was replaced by the true *chest of drawers,* the *highboy,* and the *lowboy.* A lowboy has a frame with one to three drawers, mounted on legs. A highboy is essentially a lowboy with a chest of drawers mounted on top of it.

These pieces and practically all the others made in the "period styles," which are considered on pages 23-47, were also made in pine, maple, and other local woods in country regions. There are, for instance, painted pine chairs in a much simplified interpretation of Chippendale style which we call "country Chippendale." These provincial items are unsophisticated but often skillfully made. Moreover, the native woods were sometimes worked by trained cabinetmakers into pieces as handsome and expertly built as those that were made of the costlier imported mahogany.

Painted Furniture

For some years it has been the fashion to scrape down old pine and maple furniture to the natural wood, removing the numerous coats of paint it has acquired through the years, in the belief that it is being thus "restored" to its "original" finish. Actually, however, our ancestors used paint a great deal, on their furniture and on their walls and floors. We know that windsors and slat-backs were usually painted, often a dark green or black. The chests of the 1600's and early 1700's were painted, either in a solid color or in a varicolored design, or, if they had carved decoration, with accents in red and black.

Most country-made pine of the 1700's was painted. The commonest color was "Indian red," a soft brownish red, which was inexpensively made and widely used. Pieces are sometimes found with this old faded color still on them, and it is carefully preserved by collectors. Blue was also used, and when it survives, has faded to a soft light shade. Even curly maple, which we now consider very ornamental, was sometimes covered with paint or stained to look like mahogany. While many pieces were simply given a flat coat of paint, others, especially after the mid-1700's, were painted in ornamental designs or in simulation of wood graining.

This custom continued with the Hitchcock chairs and their contemporaries of the 1820's and later. By this time stenciling had become a vogue, and was used on entire sets of bedroom furniture. It provided an inexpensive substitute for the hand painting and gilding which had been popular a little earlier on more formal furniture. Even the Grand Rapids cottage furniture was painted in light colors and trimmed with stripes and floral nosegays.

Victorian Furniture

Varied as it is, all this pine and country furniture of three centuries is still only one part of the whole furniture picture. Another consists of the more elegant and fashionable things of the 1800's which the country furniture sometimes tried to imitate—the rose-carved chairs, the horsehair sofas, the heavy sideboards, the whatnots. As we move farther away from the nineteenth century, these things are becoming more and more accepted as antiques.

All the furniture made between 1840 and 1900 has usually been lumped together under the one name Victorian because it was all made during the long reign of Queen Victoria, 1837-1901. But the Victorian is not a single style. Fashions shifted, just as they always had and always will.

Victorian designers were eclectic; that is, they selected designs and motifs from various styles of previous eras. Sometimes they tried to reproduce accurately but more often they used the old designs in new ways. Often they combined elements from unrelated styles, or applied decorative details to unrelated forms.

Gothic, Louis XV, Louis XVI, Jacobean, Renaissance, Oriental, all gave inspiration to Victorian designers at different times. So instead of calling all their furniture just Victorian, we would do well to specify its style periods. These overlapped to a certain extent, one style continuing for some time after a new one had come in, but we can establish the approximate dates when they were at their peak.

Victorian Gothic Chair, 1840's

Victorian Gothic was the earliest. It appeared in this country in the 1830's, before American Empire had run its course, and continued as late as the 1880's, but its main period was the 1840's. It was not at all like real medieval furniture, which was bulky and stiff. Victorian Gothic was mostly small and light, and its gothic character consisted only of decorative details, such as pointed arches, and tracery like that of a rose window. Gothic was never as widespread a fashion in furniture as it was in architecture, which sprinkled the country with peaked-roof houses covered with gingerbread.

Victorian Rococo Dressing Table, 1850's

Victorian Rococo Chairs, 1850's

Victorian Rococo Table, 1850's

Much more prevalent in furniture was the Victorian Rococo, which had become the style by 1840 and held first place in popularity until the 1860's. In its day it was called the "French style," for it was a conscious imitation or adaptation of the Louis XV style of the 1700's, the style known as rococo from the French words for rock and shell. This was the fashion that in the mid-1800's produced the familiar sofas, chairs, and tables in mahogany, rosewood, and black walnut, with exaggeratedly scrolled contours, curved legs, and boldly carved decoration in naturalistic motifs such as roses, grapes, leaves, and birds.

This was the style in which the famous John Belter of New York worked most. He produced quantities of rococo sofas, chairs, and tables which were shipped to all parts of the country. His process of laminating wood made it possible to bend and shape it and also to carve it in extraordinarily intricate designs.

Elaborate carving in naturalistic motifs was also a

Belter Furniture, 1850's

feature of the new furniture that emerged before this florid style had run its full course. Victorian Renaissance we may call it, since it owed its inspiration to the Italian Renaissance. It rose to popularity about 1850 and continued through the 1860's. Pieces were imposing and ponderous, with heavy carving, wide scrolled moldings, and generous use of marble. There was a consciously classic accent in the form, and sometimes in the motifs

Victorian
Renaissance
Chair, 1860's

of the carving, but the emphasis was on mass and ornamentation.

A more delicate classic influence was apparent in another style of the 1860's, a revival or adaptation of the Louis XVI. Just as that eighteenth-century style had replaced the rococo Louis XV with straight lines and restrained decoration in the classic taste, so this Victorian Classic was more delicate and simple than what had gone before.

The Victorian Jacobean had its vogue in the 1870's. Never a dominant style, it nevertheless produced a good many pieces whose chief characteristics were the use of strapwork—wide, flat, ornamental moldings in interlaced designs—and small turned spindles to form railings on shelves and table edges.

In the 1870's, too, the Oriental influence was at its height, though it continued to the end of the century. Lacquer from both China and Japan was popular, and in American furniture, fretwork, "Chinesey" carving, and bamboo were evidences of the Oriental style.

The best of all this nineteenth-century furniture was hand-made and hand-carved, according to old cabinetmaking traditions, but at the same time new manufacturing methods were putting a great deal of flimsy, second-rate furniture in these styles on the market. In the 1860's certain designers revolted against these cheap products, but they did not succeed in staying the course of the machine. Instead, ironically enough, some of their designs were adopted by manufacturers and cheaply produced.

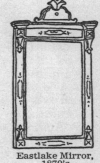

Eastlake Mirror,
1870's

That was how the Eastlake style of the 1870's originated. It was named for Charles L. Eastlake, an Englishman whose *Hints on Household Taste* and other books had a wide audience. Eastlake furniture, which shows some Gothic and Jacobean influence in its decorative details, is usually of oak or some other light wood with dark trimming. It is rectilinear in form, and ornamented with flat moldings and shallow carving in simple patterns.

Mission furniture, which came in before 1900, was another style that was machine-made. It was named for the simple early furniture of the Spanish colonial missions in the Southwest.

The Eighteenth-Century Period Styles

These phases of design, or styles, that furniture passed through during the Victorian era were really just the continuation of a process that had been going on for centuries. The historic styles of the 1700's are what we call Queen Anne, Chippendale, Hepplewhite, and Sheraton. Though these names are familiar, they are as often misunderstood as "early American," and actually they have much more specific meanings.

These names are merely convenient and accepted handles by which we identify certain broad style groups and link them with their approximate periods in history. Each style reflects the prevailing taste of its time, and since tastes change, constantly but gradually, the styles merge gradually one into another, overlapping for a number of years. The dates we use for them mark only their peak of popularity.

In broad terms these styles have followed the same trends throughout western Europe and America during the past three centuries, but each country has interpreted them in its own way. Thus we can distinguish the Louis XV style of France from the Georgian style of England which was contemporary with it, though we can also recognize a basic relationship between them.

In American furniture the major styles followed those of England, for up to the Revolution the Colonies naturally accepted the standards of the mother country, and afterward too the strongest foreign influence here was English. For that reason we use for the most part the names of English rulers and designers to designate American furniture styles.

We must remember, however, that in America the styles lagged behind those of England because of the slowness of travel and communication, and that even in England the dates do not coincide exactly. In rural districts here, and in frontier regions as the nation expanded to the westward, they lagged even further behind the more up-to-date urban centers.

That is why we can say, for instance, that the Queen Anne style period in America was from about 1725 to 1750, though the good queen had been dead and gone eleven years by the first of those dates. And some pieces in Queen Anne style were made even later than 1750, long after the style had really gone out of fashion.

After the Revolution French influence on our furniture was strong, and so we apply the names Directoire and Empire to American furniture that shows this influence. Here again, however, the dates of American Empire extend much later than the dates when Napoleon was emperor.

These period styles and their characteristics are more fully discussed later on, but you can get an idea of their sequence, dates, and relationship one to another from the following table. This must not be taken as definite and exact; it is merely a much simplified listing with approximate dates, to help orient you to the main periods in furniture design.

In connection with English furniture, you will notice, the names of the Georges are used to designate periods, as well as those of designers active at the same time. In speaking of American furniture we rather arbitrarily use the names of rulers at first, then of designers, then of rulers again.

The styles from Queen Anne to Sheraton are the ones that are most generally appreciated today. Their qualities of design have stood the test of many generations. They are the styles most widely and constantly reproduced. In form and scale they are suited to modern living, and in line and proportion they are satisfying to many tastes. Knowing something about these styles will add a great deal to your enjoyment of old furniture, and will also help you to make an intelligent selection of reproductions.

Period Styles of Furniture

Period Style	Historical Dates	Approximate Style Dates		
		IN ENGLAND	IN AMERICA	
William and Mary	1689-1702	1690-1710	1700-1725	
Queen Anne	1702-1714	1710-1720	1725-1750	
Georgian				
Early	George I, 1714-1727	1720-1730		
Middle	George II, 1727-1760	1730-1760		
Late	George III, 1760-1820	1760-1810		
	George IV, Regent, 1811-1820 }			
	George IV, King, 1820-1830 }			
Chippendale		1745-1770	1755-1790	
Adam		1760-1780		
Hepplewhite		1780-1790	1785-1800	
Sheraton		1790-1810	1795-1815	
Regency		1810-1830		
		IN FRANCE		
Directoire	1795-1799	1795-1805	1805-1815	
Empire	1804-1814	1805-1820	1810-1840	

There is a difference between recognizing a *period style* and telling whether a given piece is *of its period*. For example, a modern reproduction may be in true Chippendale style, but it is not, obviously, a piece of the Chippendale period. Learning to tell the difference requires, among other things, a knowledge of construction —how a drawer is dovetailed, how a chair leg is mortised and tenoned, and so on. We cannot go into these internal details here, but we can point out some of the external features of furniture that you need to notice in order to identify styles.

There is no one detail that declares the period of a piece, such as a foot or a carved shell; you have to take the whole piece into account. But once you develop an acquaintance with the fundamental character of a style, you will find your eye taking in general form at a glance, and then picking out the details of line and decoration. You will also observe the little differences as well as the major similarities between pieces in the same style.

The best way to learn something about furniture is to look at actual pieces, but as a guide to the chief characteristics of the different styles, turn to the itemized section farther on in this chapter. The illustrations there show the development of the major forms. Certain earmarks of style may be seen more clearly in chairs than in any other form, and the sequence of chairs shown will be helpful in identifying other pieces too.

When the first English settlers came to America, England was just emerging from the Middle Ages. Her furniture was still essentially medieval in style, heavy and cumbersome, made chiefly of oak. The early colonists naturally repeated the forms and designs they had known in England, so that our seventeenth-century furniture is really medieval in character.

By 1700 furniture had become gradually more plentiful, and new forms, new kinds of pieces, appeared to fill domestic needs. A tendency toward lighter, more graceful, more comfortable furniture also began to be apparent, and was to increase throughout the century. With the Queen Anne style which reached America about 1725 there was a distinct change from the stiff, rigid furniture of earlier periods. For the first time the straight, turned legs were replaced by more graceful, curving ones called *cabriole*. Chairs acquired rounded backs and seats, and were shaped with a new regard for comfort. Curves and scrolls appeared on the edges and frames of tables, on the skirts of highboys, on mirror frames. The most fashionable wood at this time was walnut.

Gradually this graceful and rather simple Queen Anne style in America flowered into the more elaborate rococo, following the same development that had been going on in Europe. In France the rococo style reached its peak under Louis XV. The English rococo of the mid-1700's was somewhat more subdued but characterized by the same kind of naturalistic motifs in form and decoration, based on the curve and scroll rather than the straight line.

The chief exponent of the eighteenth-century rococo in England was the great designer Thomas Chippendale,

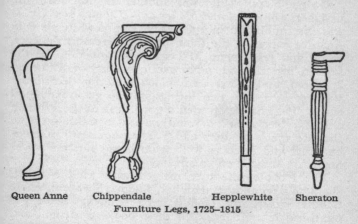

Queen Anne   Chippendale   Hepplewhite   Sheraton
Furniture Legs, 1725–1815

whose book of designs, *The Gentleman and Cabinet-maker's Director,* first appeared in 1754. Some of these designs were essentially elaborations of Queen Anne modes; many combined motifs and forms borrowed from French, Gothic, and Chinese design. Chippendale's influence was so great that his name is frequently applied to the whole style period during which his designs were popular.

In this country the Chippendale period produced much fine craftsmanship in rich designs of considerable variety. The cabriole leg was a favorite, usually terminating in a claw-and-ball foot, but straight legs were also common. The most fashionable wood was mahogany, and fine pieces were also made in walnut and in cherry. Our Chippendale is a robust style, at its best characterized by good proportions, a generous substantiality, and effective use of carved ornamentation.

In the second half of the 1700's the classic influence affected furniture design as it did the other crafts. In English home furnishings the trend from the rococo to the classic was introduced by Robert Adam and his brothers, architects and interior designers. In this country, since there is little furniture that follows Adam designs closely, it is usual to speak of the neo-classic style which succeeded Chippendale as Hepplewhite.

George Hepplewhite was another English furniture designer, whose *Cabinet Maker and Upholsterers' Guide* was first published in 1788. The Hepplewhite style in America expressed the trend toward increasing delicacy, grace, and refinement. Mahogany continued to be the favorite material, but other exotic woods like satinwood appeared, and inlays were much used for decoration. Veneers were also used increasingly to get ornamental effects. They had been used a good deal in the William and Mary period and to some extent ever since, but from the late 1700's on they had a new popularity in cross-bandings and insets as well as on broad surfaces where fine grain showed off to advantage.

The Hepplewhite style merged with what is called Sheraton after another designer, Thomas Sheraton, whose *Cabinet-maker and Upholsterer's Drawing Book* was published in 1791-1794. All these books of design, and others less well known, were used by furniture makers in this country and hence exerted a direct influence on American furniture.

It should be emphasized that the American furniture and even most of the English that is called by the names of these designers was not actually produced by them. Some of it was patterned exactly after their designs, but much of it was a free interpretation. Sometimes items are called Chippendale, for example, which have no close relation to Chippendale's designs, but which were produced while his work was fashionable and have the same general character. The designers' names are used for practical purposes to designate three successive style periods.

Early Sheraton pieces are quite similar to those called Hepplewhite, and there is no sharp dividing line between the two. Generally, pieces with slender, tapered legs and inlaid decoration are called Hepplewhite, and those with straight reeded legs and carving instead of inlay are called Sheraton. This is a convenient but not really correct distinction, since both men made designs of both types. Both were essentially neo-classic styles, and correspond to the Louis XVI style of the late 1700's in France.

About 1800 France began to exert a much stronger and more direct influence on America than before. Our own Revolution and the French Revolution established a feeling of kinship between the two countries and also opened the way for new trade relations. Americans soon developed the admiration for French taste in matters of dress, food, and the arts which has persisted to this day.

French furniture design affected America directly, as well as via England. French *émigré* cabinetmakers came to work in America, and French products were imported. But independence did not sever ties with England or wipe out our English background, and English influence continued to be dominant.

The neo-classic style which had prevailed in the late 1700's took on new features. In France it became the Directoire style, deriving its inspiration from ancient Greece. Then it merged into the Empire, which was considerably more massive and imposing, frequently using Egyptian motifs. In England the Sheraton style after 1800 gradually developed into the English counterpart of Empire, which is called Regency because it coincided with the Regency of George IV.

All these names—Directoire, Empire, late Sheraton, Regency—have been applied to American furniture of the early 1800's. Our furniture did show the influence of all four, and distinctions among them are not always clear. Some of the later pieces have been given the additional name of Greek Revival, because they coincide in style and date with the Greek Revival in architecture.

In an effort to find a distinctly American term to cover this whole neo-classic period, some people have adopted the name Early Federal. It is more usual, however, to speak of the light, refined furniture made from about 1790 to 1815 as American Sheraton; and that of about 1815-1840, which became a good deal heavier in line and coarser in detail, as American Empire.

Some American Empire closely imitated French Empire, using a good deal of marble and ormolu mounts with mahogany, but the more typical pieces made here were not so dressy. One of their characteristics is heavy, ornate carving in naturalistic forms. The flaring legs of pedestal tables, for instance, instead of being reeded or delicately carved in a leaf design as in early Sheraton, are in the form of large animal legs and paws, and further elaborated with heavy leafage and scrolls. There is also a characteristic use of heavy scrolls and curves, as in drawer fronts and upright members of case pieces, and backs and feet of sofas.

Major Forms in Period Styles

The American furniture types pictured and described here are the major ones that occur in the period styles from Queen Anne to Empire (*approximately 1725-1840*). There were many variations on these, and other forms as well, but these are the basic types.

BEDS. Before 1730 in America a bedstead was usually a simple frame strung with rope to support a mattress. It had turned posts and low head and foot, or no footboard. The word *bed,* incidentally, meant a feather bed or mattress; the frame was a *bedstead.*

Such bedsteads continued to be used in many homes into the 1800's, but among people of fashion the high-post bed was used from about 1730 until 1835. The four high posts were connected at the top by a wood frame called a *tester,* from which a *valance* was hung. Sometimes the valance was wood, carved or painted, but more often it was a fabric matching the curtains which hung at the corners. Beds of the Queen Anne period had plain turned posts or octagonal *pencil posts,* tapering toward the top. Later the foot posts were usually turned, carved, or reeded, but the head posts, being hidden by the curtains, were plain.

Chippendale, Hepplewhite, and Sheraton beds differ chiefly in details of ornamentation, and in proportions—the

Hepplewhite Field Bed, 1790's

less massive the later. The *field* or *tent bed* of the late 1700's and early 1800's had an arched frame for the canopy instead of a flat, straight-sided tester.

After about 1810 high-post beds again took on impressive dimensions, and the carving of their posts became lavish. Those with fat posts decorated with heavy leaf or pineapple carving date after 1825.

Low-post beds also appeared in the Empire period. A type borrowed from France had straight head and foot board and was placed sideways along the wall with a circular canopy attached to the wall above. From this, which was unusual in America, developed the *sleigh bed* which had low, outcurving head and foot. A more common type at this period had rather thick turned posts about five feet high, with a low scrolled headboard and a similar board or turned rail at the foot.

Victorian Rococo and Renaissance beds often had high, very ornate headboards. This was also the period of the *half-tester bed,* which had a low foot, and a canopy or tester extending only over the head. This type was particularly popular in the South. Cast-iron beds were

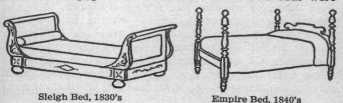

Sleigh Bed, 1830's   Empire Bed, 1840's

Victorian
Half-Tester Bed, 1860's

used from the 1860's on. Brass ones became popular in the 1880's. Most of the early beds were wide, particularly those with high posts. Twin beds did not exist much before 1900.

CHAIRS. By the early 1700's chairs were being designed with more regard to the human frame than ever before. The typical Queen Anne chair has a solid splat in the back with a yoke-shaped crest, and curved or cabriole legs. The back is curved so that it appears "spoon-shaped" when seen from the side. The legs are usually joined by a turned or shaped stretcher in New England chairs, usually not in Philadelphia ones. The feet are most often in the shape of a round pad; sometimes simply pointed; sometimes carved with a three-toed effect called *trifid*. When there are arms they are curved or flaring.

Chippendale chairs are of great variety. Characteristic are the generous proportions, the pierced and often carved back and splat with curved cresting rail coming out to points or "ears" at the corners, and the cabriole legs with claw-and-ball feet, often with carving on the knees. Straight-leg examples are also common, and so are ladder-backs which have shaped horizontal slats instead of an upright splat. The designs of splats, ladders, and carving are manifold.

Hepplewhite chair designs are almost equally varied but the fundamental form and proportions are fairly constant. They are generally lighter in appearance and have lower, narrower backs than Chippendale. The tapered leg is typical, sometimes ending in a tapered block or *spade* foot. The back is usually *shield* shape, though with a highly curved instead of straight top rail. Sometimes it is in an interlaced heart design, sometimes it has a central splat. Both types are ornamented with carving or inlay in swags, urns, feathers, or other classical

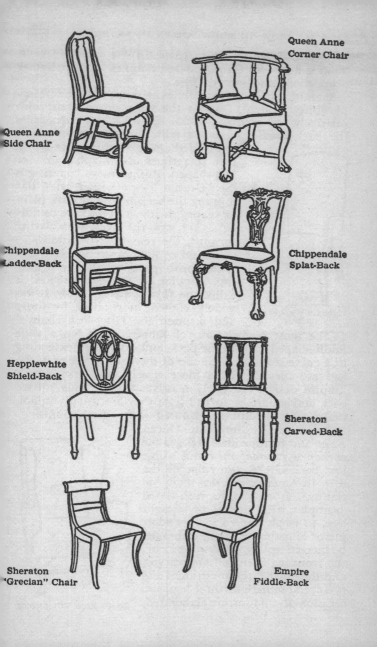

Queen Anne
Corner Chair

Queen Anne
Side Chair

Chippendale
Ladder-Back

Chippendale
Splat-Back

Hepplewhite
Shield-Back

Sheraton
Carved-Back

Sheraton
"Grecian" Chair

Empire
Fiddle-Back

motifs. Ladder-backs also occur in Hepplewhite style. They differ from Chippendale examples in their lighter proportions and tapered legs.

Sheraton chairs are usually more rectilinear than Hepplewhite, though of about the same proportions, with relatively low, narrow backs. In straight-leg examples the back usually has a straight top rail. Sometimes it

has reeded and turned posts or balusters, sometimes also a splat, urn- or lyre-shaped. Rather more common is the "Grecian" type with a wide slat topping the back and other slats, plain or shaped, below it. This type usually has *saber* legs, the front ones flaring forward, the rear ones backward.

A kind of light, graceful piece decorated with painting and even gilding, popular in the early 1800's, is called the *Sheraton fancy chair*. It was widely copied in country furniture and inspired the Hitchcock chair.

Martha Washington Chair

The most typical form of Empire chair has a wide fiddle-shaped splat in the back, and side pieces extending in a curve from the wide top of the back to the seat; the legs are curved. Chairs more closely following French Empire design are fairly massive, with a wide square back and square or turned legs; they are usually upholstered and sometimes decorated with brass mounts.

An attractive form in Queen Anne and Chippendale styles is the *corner* or *roundabout chair,* whose low back circles two sides of the seat. In America this saw many variations, from simple rush-seated examples with turned or straight legs, to richly carved Chippendale pieces of mahogany with elaborately pierced splats. Most often only the front leg is curved and carved, and the other three are straight and plain; but sometimes three legs, and occasionally all four, are elaborated.

Queen Anne Wing Chair

The *open-arm chair* with completely up-holstered back and seat was made in America from the Chippendale period on. Chippendale

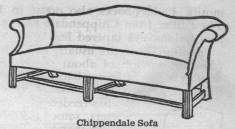

Chippendale Sofa

examples are fairly broad and solid, and usually have straight grooved legs. Hepplewhite and Sheraton examples, called *Martha Washington chairs,* are slenderer and have a proportionately higher back. Legs are tapered and often inlaid, or turned and perhaps reeded.

Wing chairs, called easy chairs in their day, were

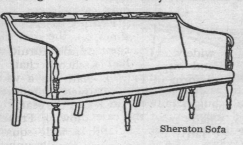

made from the Queen Anne period on. Queen Anne ones have high backs, and the arms are formed in a vertical roll. Chippendale and Hepple-

Sheraton Sofa

white ones are relatively broader in the back, and the roll of the arms is horizontal. Legs and feet follow the variations of each style.

Seats of chairs in the formal styles are usually upholstered. In all these periods both removable slip seats and seats upholstered over the frame occur. Designs and types of fabrics follow as definite changes in styles as the chairs on which they are used.

Sofas and *settees* are really enlarged chairs, and in general follow chair design. Queen Anne and Chippendale upholstered sofas are like extended wing chairs. There are also chair-back settees: only the seat is upholstered, and the back looks like two or three carved chair backs in a row. These are much rarer in American furniture than in English.

CHESTS OF DRAWERS are the major group of what are called *case pieces*, which comprise also desks, highboys, and other forms which have a case or frame.

Early chests of drawers, 1690 to 1725, were simple and functional, usually with ball-shaped feet, round or slightly elongated. Queen Anne examples with cabriole legs are rare. Chippendale chests of drawers sometimes have *claw-and-ball* feet but a *bracket* foot is more usual, its con-

Hepplewhite Chest of Drawers

tour an *ogee* or S-shaped curve. In the Hepplewhite period a simpler bracket, single-curved or straight, was used. By the Sheraton period, turned or reeded legs replaced brackets on most case pieces.

From Chippendale times on, the case of a chest of drawers often had a curved *bow* or *serpentine* front. A rare Chippendale form is *bombé* or *kettle-based,* in which the lower part of the frame, drawers and all, bulges outward in an ogee curve.

A specialized treatment of the case called the *block-front* was produced in New England from the 1760's through the 1780's. The smooth front is broken by large raised panels, or blocks, extending the height of the piece, with a large carved shell at the top of the block. This treatment was applied to highboys, chests-on-chest, desks, secretaries, and dressing tables as well as to chests of drawers. The blockfront type reached its

Blockfront Chest of Drawers

highest development at the hands of the Goddards and Townsends, cabinetmakers of Newport, Rhode Island. It was also made in Massachusetts and Connecticut.

Detail of hardware

Sheraton
Chest of Drawers

The eighteenth-century chests usually had four drawers but taller ones were made, particularly in the country, with six or more graduated drawers. Such a piece is often called a *high-daddy*.

A *chest-on-chest* was just what the name implies—one chest of drawers upon another; the type was made chiefly in the Chippendale period.

Shortly after 1800 appeared the first chests of drawers with mirrors attached instead of being hung on the wall above. Typical Empire bureaus have heavy scrolls and curves in the upright members, drawer fronts, and feet.

CLOCKS are timepieces, primarily, rather than just furniture. Their cases, however, represent a branch of the cabinetmaker's work, and as such they are considered here, without reference to their mechanism. The form of the clock case changed with the development of the mechanism, but it also showed in many features the development of styles that affected all furniture.

The *tall clock,* affectionately known as the *grandfather clock,* was made here throughout the 1700's and half of the 1800's. Earliest examples had a flat top with rather heavy cornice, above a square dial. About 1725 the arched top appeared, with the top of the dial arched to correspond.

The scroll top was developed in the Chippendale period, along with the scroll-top highboy, secretary, and mirror. Examples vary greatly in elaboration of the case and also of the dial.

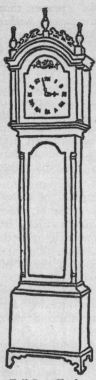

Tall-Case Clock,
1800

The influence of Hepplewhite and Sheraton may be seen in decorative details and slenderer proportions near the end of the century, but the scroll top persisted to about 1800. After that, examples with arched top surmounted by fretwork were in vogue. American grandfather clocks are often difficult to date exactly.

Up to about 1770 dials are of brass, with a silvered ring on which the numerals are engraved. After that date appears the painted, or enameled, dial, usually of iron, sometimes of pewter. On brass dials, the spandrels (the pie-shaped corner pieces) are often decorated with applied ornaments cast in bronze. Dials with a moon face in the upper part, made between about 1760 and 1810, have arrangements worked by the inner mechanism for telling the days of the week or the month. Dials and parts of the mechanism were frequently imported from England. The name that usually appears on a clock face is that of the maker of the mechanism, not necessarily of the case.

Small clocks in the form of tall clocks but only four feet high, more or less, were made in the late 1700's and early 1800's. These miniature grandfathers are called *grandmother clocks*.

The function of the tall clock's long case was to house the long pendulum and the weights. But clocks could be made with a short pendulum, and driven by springs instead of weights. *Bracket clocks* had been made in England as early as grandfather clocks. In this country *wall* and *mantel* or *shelf clocks* were made chiefly from about 1800 on, when the

English
Bracket Clock,
mid-1700's

Pillar-and-Scroll
Mantel Clock,
early 1800's

use of wooden works, cheaper than brass ones, put timepieces within financial reach of a wide market.

The popular-priced mantel clock is the contribution of Eli Terry, of Plymouth, Connecticut. The early Terry case, called the *pillar and scroll,* looked like the top section of a tall clock, with a scroll top, side columns or pillars, scrolled skirt, and bracket feet, a square enameled dial, and below it a scene painted on glass. This form was also used by other makers of the period.

Mantel clocks gradually took other, and less graceful forms. Some had heavier side columns and less flowing scroll tops. The cases were occasionally decorated with stenciling. A common type of the 1840's is the plain rectangular veneered wood case, with a painted panel below the dial. The familiar *steeple clock* is of the 1840's and 1850's.

The *banjo clock,* designed to hang on the wall with a small gilt bracket to support it, was devised and patented in 1802 by Simon Willard of Roxbury, Massachusetts. He and his brother Aaron are also famous for fine tall-case and mantel clocks. Examples of the banjo type were made by numerous others, not all of whom put their names on their clocks. The frame, in the shape of a banjo, is gilt. It usually has a finial in the form of an eagle or other motif above the round dial, brass brackets beside the long center panel, and painted decoration there and on the rectangular glass panel of the bottom section.

Clocks for wall or mantel were made in an increasing variety of fanciful shapes from the 1840's on. They are known by such descriptive names as *acorn, hourglass, lyre,* and the like. Cases were made in cast iron, bronze, marble, papier-maché inset with mother-of-pearl, and exotic woods.

Banjo
Clock,
early 1800's

Chippendale
Slant-Top Desk
with detail of hardware

DESKS AND SECRETARIES. The few desks of the 1600's were simply slant-top boxes in which writing materials were kept, and of which the closed lid served as a writing surface. They were larger and heavier than the portable desk boxes of two centuries later, which were made in rosewood or walnut and neatly fitted with little compartments. By the early 1700's those early *desk boxes* came to be attached to a supporting frame instead of being set on a table, but such *desks-on-frame* are rare.

Presently the familiar slant-top desk was evolved. The interior was fitted with drawers and pigeon-holes. The frame became a chest of drawers.

The typical fall-front desk of the Chippendale period is often called a *Governor Winthrop desk*—quite erroneously; though there were several governors named Winthrop, they all lived a good century before this type came into existence. Eighteenth-century desks often are quite simple outside but may have elaborate interiors.

While slant-top desks continued as the usual form, a new type called the *tambour desk* developed in the Hepplewhite period. It has a flat folding leaf for writing instead of the fall front, and there is a

Hepplewhite Tambour Desk
with detail of hardware

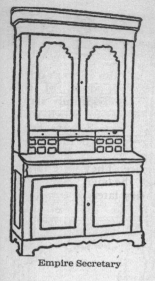

Empire Secretary

low cabinet above closed by a sliding front known as a tambour. This is composed of thin strips of wood fastened to a canvas backing so that it can roll up.

When the cabinetmaker mounted a bookcase or cabinet on top of his desk, it became a *secretary*. In Chippendale examples the cabinet doors are usually paneled wood, and the piece often has an arched top like a highboy. Hepplewhite and Sheraton secretaries are more likely to have small glass panes in the doors, and they may have flat or low scrolled tops. Later pieces have larger glass panes or wood panels in the doors.

The large flat-topped desk with two side tiers of drawers, called a *pedestal* or *kneehole desk,* is an English type of the 1750's and later, and was rarely if ever made in America. The so-called kneehole type made in America was on a smaller scale, and the two tiers of drawers, instead of being separated in the middle, had a recessed cupboard between them. The form occurs chiefly in blockfront design, and was often intended originally as a dressing table rather than a desk.

HIGHBOYS AND LOWBOYS first appeared in the William and Mary period and reached their highest development in the Chippendale, after which they went out of fashion. The lowboy consists of a few drawers in a frame on high legs. The highboy is like it, with an additional case of drawers on top. In the 1700's a low-

Queen Anne Lowboy

boy was called a *dressing table* and a highboy a *high chest*,  and both were originally bedroom pieces.

Queen Anne highboys have simple cabriole legs and usually a flat top. Chippendale highboys have cabriole legs, claw-and-ball feet, and an arched or scrolled top sometimes called a *bonnet top*. Frequently they have carving on the top and bottom drawer fronts and on the knees, heavy molding on the arched top, carved finials, and elaborate brasses. Those of Philadelphia are particularly admired for their sound proportions and rich carving.

Chippendale Highboy with detail of hardware

Examples of matching highboy and lowboy are known but they are rare. Incidentally, don't mistake for a lowboy the bottom of a highboy that has lost its superstructure: a true lowboy is smaller and lower than the lower case of a highboy.

MIRRORS. The earliest mirrors, or *looking glasses* as they were called, used in America are rare.  Large sheets of glass were unobtainable, so that in long Queen Anne mirrors the glass is in two sections. The frame is a simple wide molding with the characteristic cyma or S-curve in the upper section.

Scrolled mahogany looking-glass frames, called *fretwork*, or *silhouette mirrors*, are typical of the Chippendale period. Their silhouettes vary in intricacy. Sometimes a carved or gilded ornament is applied to the cresting.

Chippendale Fretwork Mirror

English mirrors of the time, and a few made in America, are rectangular with scrolled top, often with a gilt ornament on top and gilding on the mahogany veneer of the frame. Hepplewhite ones, mahogany and gilt, are more delicate than Chippendale and sometimes have an upper panel with a painted scene or design.

Sheraton mirrors are usually gilded, and are rectangular without the cresting ornament of previous styles. A familiar gilded type, often called *Constitution* or *tabernacle,* has a row of balls just under the top or cornice, and a painted upper

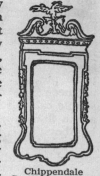

Chippendale
Scroll-Top Mirror

panel. Frequently the panel has a picture of the frigate *Constitution* doing battle in the War of 1812.

Of about the same time is the convex mirror with round gilt frame surmounted by an eagle or other ornament, and with candle brackets at the bottom. Most examples of this type, called a *girandole* mirror, were imported.

Typical mirrors of the 1820's and 1840's are rectangular, with the frame painted, stenciled, or gilded. Some examples of them have a panel above the mirror decorated with a stencil, or a painting on glass, or a relief in plaster or wood. Others have two mirror panels.

Sheraton Constitution
Mirror

The *courting mirror* has a simple frame of wood and the looking glass is surrounded by small pieces of glass with painted flowers or other decorations. The type is believed to have come from China, and to date about the year 1800.

Sheraton Convex Mirror

Hepplewhite Sideboard, with detail of hardware

SIDEBOARDS were a new form in the Hepplewhite and Sheraton periods. Previously side tables had been used for serving. The ancestor of the sideboard in England was a long, narrow, high table without drawers, flanked by a pair of cabinets. From this combination of three separable units it was but a step to the more convenient single piece combining flat surface, drawers, and cupboards in one unit.

American Hepplewhite and Sheraton sideboards vary considerably in size and shape, ranging from tidy little bow-front or straight-front pieces to long serpentine fronts. The earlier examples usually have tapered legs and ornamental inlay. Later ones are deeper, or at least have deep ends, with reeded legs and carved decoration.

American Empire sideboards sometimes combine mirrors, marble, and ormolu with mahogany, as in French Empire furniture which largely influenced their design. More characteristic are those with heavy carving in naturalistic forms.

TABLES. One of the new forms that appeared in the Queen Anne period was the tea table, devised to cater to the new fad for drinking the exotic Oriental beverage. The small table with a tilt top and pedestal base supported on three feet, called *pedestal*

Queen Anne
Tea Table

or *tripod table*, appeared in this period and has been made ever since. Rectangular tea tables were also made with cabriole legs.

Chippendale Pedestal Table

Queen Anne tables occur in many sizes, round, oval, or rectangular, with or without drop leaves. When the legs are not cabriole, they are round and tapering and end in pad feet. Some examples are fairly large, but most Queen Anne tables are small.

Chippendale pedestal tables often have carving on the base and a *scrolled* or *piecrust* edge on the top. The top sometimes revolves by means of a *birdcage* arrangement under it.

Drop-leaf or *Pembroke tables* and *card tables* are characteristic forms in the Chippendale, Hepplewhite, and Sheraton periods. Their legs and decoration are representative of their period style. Pembroke tables usually have folding slides to support the leaves. In card tables the top is in two leaves hinged together so that one folds over the other when closed; when open, a leg swings out to support it.

Chippendale Card Table

Large dining tables are rare before the Hepplewhite and Sheraton periods. Examples in those styles are often in three parts—two semicircular or oval ends and a central piece with drop leaves.

The pedestal form was used in Sheraton tables of various sizes, from small ones like the earlier tea tables to large ones for dining. This is a favorite form for dining tables today.

Another version of the Sheraton pedestal type which was made in England but is popular in America is the *drum table,* with drawers in its round, deep top.

Numerous small useful forms like sewing tables also made their appearance in the Sheraton period, and continued into the Empire.

Hepplewhite Pembroke Table

Empire pedestal tables were heavier than Sheraton and often ornamented with naturalistic carving.

FURNITURE HARDWARE. Handles or pulls on drawers in the earliest American chests were small wooden knobs, and on simple pieces knobs were occasionally used up to the 1800's. Pieces in the period styles of the 1700's and early 1800's, however, usually had brass handles. Styles in brasses changed with styles in furniture. Several types are illustrated with pieces on which they are appropriately used.

In the William and Mary period, the brass plate or escutcheon attached to the wood was small, decoratively shaped, and sometimes engraved, and the pull was a little brass *drop.* In the Queen Anne period a *bail,* or metal loop, became more usual, and the escutcheon was larger. Chippendale brasses were often very ornamental and did

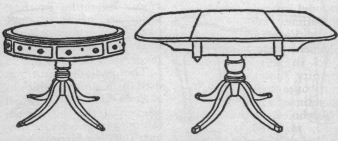

Sheraton Drum Table   Sheraton Pedestal Table

Sheraton Sewing Tables

a great deal to dress up a piece of furniture. The large plate of so-called *willow* brasses had scrolled contours, and was sometimes also pierced in a decorative design; the handle was a bail. Bails were also attached by two small round or oval plates, one at each end. Hepplewhite and Sheraton brasses usually have a bail hanging from an oval or octagonal plate stamped with a design, such as an eagle or an urn. On Empire furniture the plate was often round and stamped with a lion mask, and had a ring hanging from the lion's nose instead of an oval bail. Brass knobs with stamped designs were also used on Sheraton and Empire pieces.

At the same time on the simpler furniture flat wooden knobs were often used; they were larger and flatter than those on the early chests. Later in the 1800's wooden handles shaped in leaf or other naturalistic forms were common.

In the late 1700's and early 1800's escutcheons and knobs were occasionally of enamel instead of brass, and sometimes knobs were of ivory. Very rarely silver or Sheffield plate handles were used in this country. On country pieces, particularly early ones, bail handles were sometimes wrought of iron.

Keyhole escutcheons, when used, matched handles or knobs in design and material.

Empire Pedestal Table

Regional Types and Local Styles

While American colonial furniture largely followed English design, there was from the beginning the added influence of the new environment, and also of the settlers from other countries who brought their native traditions with them. Thus the American craftsman developed an individuality of his own and the furniture he made has an American character that distinguishes it from English.

By and large, it is simpler. Usually it adapts English designs rather than copying them exactly, and sometimes it shows innovations in both form and decoration that have no English prototypes. The butterfly table, for instance, is a typically American form. So is the block-front furniture with its shell decoration, made in New England in the 1760's to 1780's. The American Chippendale highboy became quite different from the English. On the other hand, there are certain forms in English furniture which were not made here at all.

As one new style followed another in American furniture, the first examples were made by skilled craftsmen of the leading cities and towns, and there each style reached its highest development. Until well into the 1800's these centers were relatively isolated, and there were many regional differences in their craftsmanship.

New England Queen Anne chairs, for example, are more restrained than the Queen Anne chairs of Philadelphia, and have different treatment of shell decoration and stretchers. The Hepplewhite furniture of Baltimore is different from that of New York, particularly in its lavish use of inlay.

As the frontier moved westward, carrying the Eastern styles with it, new regional characteristics developed. Hepplewhite and Sheraton furniture made in the Ohio and Mississippi Valleys is often simpler and heavier in scale than that of New England or Pennsylvania and is, moreover, as much as thirty years later. Still, despite these minor regional differences the basic styles are usually quite recognizable.

Two forms common in the South in the late 1700's and

early 1800's were unknown in the North. These are the *huntboard* and the *sugar chest*. The former is simply a high sideboard, with or without a drawer or two. Examples are usually in native woods, often southern pine. They are country-made pieces, most often in a simplified version of the Hepplewhite or Sheraton design.

Sugar chests were made for the purpose their name implies, for storing sugar and keeping it safely under lock and key. They vary a good deal in form, some being simply low, flat chests, while later ones are often little cabinets on stands. Usually they have two compartments, for white sugar and brown.

Some of the people who came here from other countries developed local styles which are apart from the main stream of period styles but which are no less a part of our furniture picture. Of these the most conspicuous are the Pennsylvania Germans, and of their furniture the most conspicuous pieces are the painted chests. Made here from the early 1700's until the mid-1800's, these perpetuated an old European tradition, with their gaily colored decoration in characteristic motifs of flowers, hearts, birds, angels, unicorns.

While the Pennsylvania "Dutch" loved color and used it lavishly, they also made much unpainted furniture in walnut and pine which has a more Continental than English character. There are unpainted chests with bracket or ball feet on a molded base; tall wide dressers with open shelves above and doors below; stretcher tables

Pennsylvania German
Painted Chest, late 1700's

with a drawer, or two drawers side by side, and widely overhanging top; trestle tables; hanging cupboards; and huge cupboards with two paneled doors, deep molded cornice and great ball feet.

The Dutch who first settled New York left their influence on furniture of the Hudson Valley, particularly in a form called the *kas*. It is similar to those great cupboards of Pennsylvania, for such pieces were common in both Holland and Germany. A very few of the New York examples have painted decoration on the doors.

The Scandinavians in the Northwest also brought painted chests, cupboards, and other pieces with them from Europe and made similar ones here. Unlike the Pennsylvania chests, the Scandinavian type has a curved lid, and the sides taper in toward the bottom. The painting is gaily colored and usually covers the entire piece more freely than on the Pennsylvania ones, where it is often arranged in neat panels.

In the Southwest, the region originally settled by the Spaniards had its local type of furniture based on Spanish designs. Eighteenth-century examples of these chests, chairs, and tables are rare but a few are preserved in local museums and churches. The type is locally reproduced today, more faithfully than it was in the adapted Mission style of the 1890's.

The religious sect called Shakers, who came here from England in the 1770's and eventually established self-contained communities in New England, New York State, Ohio, and Kentucky, developed a distinctive type of furniture for their own use. In the 1800's they also produced chairs for sale.

Shaker furniture appeals strongly to modern taste because it is extremely simple and functional, clean-lined, devoid of ornament, and very soundly built. It was made in light-colored native woods, occasionally painted red or blue. The Shaker chairs are plain slat-backs, with or without arms and rockers. The later commercial ones were sometimes of mahogany, and had seats of woven tapes. Shaker furniture is not plentiful and much of it is today in public or private collections.

Imported Furniture

While Americans have always made the greater part of their furniture, there has always been furniture imported for use here. In colonial days it came from England, and more was used in the South than elsewhere. In the 1800's furniture was imported from both France and England, though most of our "French style" furniture was made here. With the growth of antique collecting in the twentieth century, early furniture has been brought here from practically all the countries of Europe, and many of the European styles are reproduced in modern furniture.

In the early 1900's there was a taste for the elegant French and Italian styles, and for the earlier types of English. Now there are many collectors of eighteenth-century English, and finer examples are coming to this country than ever before. Among the most popular of the less formal types are French provincial, which is to Louis XV and XVI what our "country furniture" is to Chippendale and Hepplewhite; and Biedermeier, which is the provincial German equivalent of Empire.

The Orient too has provided furniture which has appealed to the catholic tastes of Americans. In the 1800's the Far Eastern trade brought exotic pieces from China and India. Today the old Chinese is again admired, and is emulated in our "Chinese modern."

The furniture actually made and used in America has a personal appeal to most Americans, however, which even the finest of other types can never have.

American Cabinetmakers

Here are a few of the more familiar names of the makers of American furniture, with their locations and working dates. In some cases we know from records when a cabinetmaker began to work and when he died or retired from the craft—such records as old city directories and church registers, bills of sale, dated pieces of furniture. In others, dates are only approximate. These are indicated by c. (for *circa,* about).

Thomas Affleck	*Philadelphia*	1763-1795
Michael Allison	*New York City*	1800-1845
Stephen Badlam	*Dorchester Lower Mills, Mass.*	1776-1815
John Belter	*New York City*	1844-1867
Thomas Burling	*New York City*	1773-1801
Aaron Chapin	*E. Windsor, Conn.*	1774-c.1798
Eliphalet Chapin	*E. Windsor, Conn.*	c.1771-1795
Henry Connelly	*Philadelphia*	1801-1826
Thomas Dennis	*Ipswich, Mass.*	c.1675-1690
Nicholas Disbrowe	*Hartford, Conn.*	c.1637-c.1683
Matthew Egerton, Jr.	*New Brunswick, N. J.*	c.1760-1802
Thomas Elfe	*Charleston, S. C.*	c.1750-1775
Benjamin Frothingham	*Charlestown, Mass.*	c.1776- ?
John Goddard	*Newport, R. I.*	1748-1783
Jonathan Gostelowe	*Philadelphia*	1770-1793
Lambert Hitchcock	*Hitchcocksville, Conn.*	c. 1820-1840's
Charles Honoré Lannuier	*New York City*	1805-1819
Prudent Mallard	*New Orleans*	1838-1879
Samuel McIntire (carver and architect)	*Salem, Mass.*	c.1776-1795
Duncan Phyfe	*New York City*	1795-1847
Benjamin Randolph	*Philadelphia*	c.1750-1780
William Savery	*Philadelphia*	1742-1787
François Seignouret	*New Orleans*	1822-1853
John Seymour	*Boston*	1796- ?
Thomas Seymour	*Boston*	1805-1828
John Shaw	*Annapolis, Md.*	1773-1794
Job Townsend	*Newport, R. I.*	1699-1765
Thomas Tufft	*Philadelphia*	1766-1794

3. *China*

Everyone knows what china is—the tableware that we use every time we eat a meal. The name covers all kinds of dishes, from the thick white mugs on a quick-lunch counter to the fine gilded plates on a lace dinner cloth. It is even used for such a variety of other things as buttons, lamps, decorative figures, doorknobs—made in New Jersey or California, in England, Mexico, Japan. The one thing they have in common is that they are all made from clay.

Two hundred and fifty years ago china had a much more limited meaning. It referred to the porcelain wares made in the country of China which were imported to Europe. A little later it referred also to the wares made in Europe in imitation of Chinese porcelain. Gradually the word has taken on the added meaning it has today, and its origin has been almost forgotten.

But this name which we use so freely that it scarcely needs to be defined is not a really specific term. The proper name for all the products of the potter's craft is *ceramics*. These are far more varied today than they were when this continent was settled, but even then there were many different kinds.

Early Pottery

A colonist emigrating from Europe to America in 1650 could have brought with him stoneware from Germany, delft from Holland, faience from France, and slipware from England. He would have found potters here, ready to supply him with crocks, bowls, and dishes of redware.

All these are different kinds of pottery. They differ in the clay used to make the *body* of a piece, in the method of firing which makes it hard, in the *glaze* that gives it a non-porous surface, and in the way it is decorated to make it attractive. But they are all alike in being made of baked clay.

The making of pottery goes back to the Garden of Eden, if Eve ever made a mud pie and baked it in the sun. The simplest kind is made by shaping clay into the desired form, by hand or on a potter's wheel, and baking it in an oven, or *kiln*. This has been done virtually everywhere from time immemorial, and is still done today, but through the ages potters have learned many ways to make their wares more useful, more durable, and more decorative.

By the time the first colonists came to America, the countries of Europe had developed several basic types of pottery. These were made from local natural clays so that each was more or less typical of its own region.

The German type was *stoneware,* which is hard and non-porous. The degree of hardness depends on the ingredients and on the degree of heat at which the ware is fired or baked in the kiln. The commonest kinds of stoneware are gray or brown, and Germany also developed a red stoneware in the natural terra-cotta color of the clay used. Some stoneware is artificially colored.

When stoneware is glazed, it is done by throwing salt into the kiln during the firing. The salt burns to a vapor which is deposited as a shiny, somewhat pitted coating on the surface of the ware.

In Holland the typical pottery was a softer ware which was given a non-porous surface by being dipped in a *tin glaze,* or *tin enamel* as it is generally called. This was a liquid mixture of clay and other materials including oxide of tin, and when fired it formed an opaque, milky-white coating. It was decorated with designs painted on in colors, especially blue and purple.

Tin-enamel pottery of this kind was made in other places besides Holland, but because the Dutch town of Delft was a great pottery-making center in the 1600's and later, it is all called *delftware.*

In England the traditional pottery was *slipware*. This was a porous ware made of buff or red clays, and covered with a *lead glaze,* containing oxide of lead among its variable ingredients. A lead glaze may be transparent and colorless, or nearly so, or it may be artificially colored. Slip-

Slipware

ware is so called because it is decorated by trailing or pouring *slip,* which is white liquid clay, over the surface.

Pottery of this kind was also decorated with designs scratched through the glaze. This type of decoration is

Sgraffito Ware

known by the Italian word for scratched, *sgraffito.* Often sgraffito and slip decoration are used together.

These were the main types of pottery familiar to the early settlers who came from Europe to America. Here they found good clays, and at a very early date potters began to work here, making simple wares for a variety of domestic needs.

Most of the local clays were red or buff, the kind to produce porous earthenware that was surfaced with a lead glaze. Often colored glazes gave rich, mottled effects in shades of green, red, yellow, and brown. Sometimes the ware was decorated with slip or sgraffito designs. Sgraffito work was done particularly in Pennsylvania, where striking and amusing designs were made with figure, flower, and bird motifs.

Suitable clays for stoneware were found in the region that is now New

Gray Stoneware

Jersey and New York. They were used there, and carried also to other localities, to make gray and brown jugs and crocks, often decorated with designs in blue.

Not much of our early native pottery is left today. Probably there is not a single piece intact that was made before 1700, and there is very little made before the Revolution. It was perishable, and it was given hard use.

But there must have been vast quantities of it made. Potters were active all over the Colonies, and people could obtain a ready supply of plates, mugs, platters, and bowls to use on their tables along with the woodenware and pewter that were also available. There were dishes for cooking and baking, utensils for the dairy and the bedroom.

These utilitarian wares were simple and sturdy in shape, naïve and colorful in decoration. They were also rather heavy, and sometimes quite crude.

For their finer china, Americans relied on imports from Europe, as they did for their finer glassware—and as, indeed, they have continued to do to this day. From the early 1700's, the new wares that were being devised abroad were admired here, and imported increasingly throughout the century. The English potters in particular found a good market in America, so good that after the Revolution they began creating designs especially to appeal to American tastes.

By 1700 English potters were experimenting with wares different from their traditional slipware, adapting types made on the Continent. These were salt-glaze stoneware, borrowed from Germany; delft, from Holland; and redware, which was brought to England from Holland and had also been made in Germany.

English salt-glaze is light in weight and has a characteristic grayish color. It was often fashioned in molds to give it unusual shapes and decoration in relief. Sometimes it had simple "scratch-blue" decoration. Occasionally it was painted in colors.
English delft was painted

Salt-Glaze Stoneware,
early 1700's

Delftware, early 1700's

in blue, purple, or polychrome on the milky-white tin glaze. The designs of flowers, figures, or landscapes were often copied from the Chinese.

The redware brought from Holland was a hard, unglazed stoneware. The English made a little of that type, but used the red clay much more to make the softer earthenware, which they coated with lead glazes.

Besides these adopted types, English potters developed a number of *variegated wares*. Their mottled or streaked colors were achieved either by mixed colored clays, in which case they are called *agate* wares; or by colored lead glazes, which produced *marbled* wares. Some of the marbled wares go by such descriptive names as *combed* and *tortoiseshell*.

These were the wares brought from England to the Colonies up to the time of the Revolution. In addition, delftware was imported from Holland, especially in the form of tiles, like those shown at the heading of this chapter. These were much used for framing fireplaces. A certain amount of German stoneware was known here too.

All these types belong under the broad classification of *pottery*. This includes both the hard, non-porous stoneware, and the softer, porous earthenware. The other broad classification of ceramics is *porcelain*. A fundamental distinction between the two is that pottery is opaque and porcelain is translucent, and the simplest way to tell one from the other is to hold them up to a strong light.

Porcelain

Porcelain did not figure in European ceramic history until the 1700's. When it did, it affected the whole course of its development.

Europeans first became acquainted with porcelain when it was brought from China in the days of Marco

Polo. As trade with the Orient developed from the 1500's on, porcelain was one of the exotic delights that Europeans most admired. It was far more exquisite than any of their own ceramics. Not only was it white, thin, light in weight, delicate in decoration, but it also had the virtue of being hard and non-porous.

Porcelain had been made in China for hundreds of years, but the way it was made was a secret to Europeans. Potters, chemists, glassmakers experimented in vain to discover the mystic formula.

Not until 1709 did one succeed, an alchemist named Johann Friedrich Boettger. His discovery led to the establishment of a porcelain manufactory at Meissen, a few miles from Dresden in Saxony. Eventually the ware came to be produced all over the continent of Europe.

Meanwhile the influence of China affected most other kinds of ceramics as well. Potters who were not trying to compete with porcelain were at least trying to imitate some of its desirable qualities.

The secret of porcelain making which had been so elusive was found to lie in two essential ingredients. The Chinese names for them are kaolin and petuntse. We call them china clay and china stone. These are necessary to produce a ware with the distinctive hard, white, translucent, vitreous character of Chinese porcelain. Such a ware is called *hard-paste* or "true" porcelain. The *paste* is the clay body of the ware, as distinguished from the glassy surface or glaze.

The materials used in the glaze of hard-paste porcelain are closely related to those of the paste, and the two are fired at the same time. Thus they become so fused that along the edge of a broken piece you can hardly tell where one ends and the other begins. This is in contrast with most other wares, where, along a broken edge, the glaze is clearly visible as a separate coating.

In their attempts to make a ware with the attractive qualities of Oriental porcelain, European potters experimented with mixing the materials of glass with clay, to make the body, and covering it with a lead glaze. What they produced was something of a cross between a translucent pottery and an opaque glass. It was hard, white, translucent, and vitreous, but it was not "true" porcelain either in ingredients or in the method of making it.

This glassy type of porcelain, which had various modifications during the eighteenth century, is called *soft-paste* or "artificial" porcelain. It is not really soft, of course. To the eye and touch it is as hard as true porcelain, and there is no quick and easy way by which you can positively tell the one from the other at a glance.

The word soft-paste, incidentally, is too often misused today. It should be applied only to certain kinds of porcelain and never to pottery, even though pottery does look softer.

Within fifty years after porcelain production started at Meissen, other factories were established to make hard-paste ware at Furstenburg, Höchst, Ludwigsburg, Nymphenburg, Frankenthal, and Berlin in Germany, and at Vienna in Austria. In France there were factories making soft-paste ware at St. Cloud, Vincennes, Chantilly, and Mennecy-Villeroy by the mid-1700's. The Sèvres works, which absorbed the Vincennes factory, made soft-paste originally but by 1769 was making hard-paste.

Meissen
Porcelain, 1735

In England porcelain was being made in the mid-1700's at Bow, Chelsea, Derby, and Worcester. These English wares are all soft-paste. Though they often imitated Meissen models, they and the French soft-paste have a delicacy and charm all their own.

While the development of earthenware and stoneware during the eighteenth century was from the rather coarse and humble toward the more refined and versatile, porcelain

Chelsea Porcelain, 1755

on the other hand started at the top of the ladder. From the beginning its production on the Continent was under the sponsorship of rulers, and it was the plaything of the aristocracy. The exquisite, fragile, difficult material seemed ideally suited to express the tastes of the period, and was treated as ornamental rather than utilitarian.

Porcelain was, to be sure, made in tea, chocolate, and dinner services, and many other usable forms, but these were sometimes very ornate. There was, for instance, the famous "swan" dinner service made at Meissen in the 1740's for Count Brühl, director of the works. It had over 700 pieces, and each one was elaborately decorated with beautifully modeled swans or other water creatures, some of them in bas-relief, some completely in the round.

Flowers modeled in full relief, exquisitely formed and colored, were sprinkled so lavishly over dishes and other objects that such decoration is called *flower encrustation*. This was done at Meissen and most other porcelain factories in the 1700's, and it was very popular in the first half of the 1800's too.

Ceramic Figures

Porcelain was made in many forms that had no purpose but to be decorative. A major product was figures, ranging in height from a few inches to twenty or thirty, and great virtuosity went into their modeling. Making them was an intricate process, for arms, legs, and other parts were all fashioned in separate molds and then assembled. The subjects varied from romanticized shepherds and shepherdesses in floral bowers, portraits of actual people, characters from the Italian Comedy, mythological personages, to birds, flowers, and animals—singly and in groups.

The fondness for figures was not, however, limited to porcelain. In Staffordshire, especially, many were made in pottery, with colored glazes. In these too the subjects were persons real and imaginary, animals and birds. A favorite is the jolly, rotund figure modeled in the form of a pitcher, called a *Toby jug*.

Decorative Techniques

Many of the eighteenth-century wares, both pottery and porcelain, show strong Chinese influence in form and especially in ornamentation. The wares actually made in China which came to Europe, on the other hand, often showed European influence, for by the mid-1700's the huge trade in Oriental export porcelain, made to special order, had begun.

Painted decoration on European wares was often in blue alone, like the blue-and-white Chinese ware. Painted motifs were frequently *chinoiseries*—Europeanized versions of Chinese flowers, figures, or scenes. There was also decoration in conscious imitation of certain Japanese types, called Imari and Kakiemon.

Painting is probably the most versatile kind of decoration on both pottery and porcelain, for it may range from a few blue splotches to an exquisite landscape in sixteen different colors. At its best it is a highly specialized art, and there were many decorators of the 1700's whose work is recognizable by its style.

The pigments used in ceramic painting are metallic compounds which are applied sometimes under the glaze, sometimes over it. Some of the *overglaze* colors are called *enamels. Gilding* is also applied over the glaze, as are the various metallic compounds which produce *copper, gold,* and *silver luster.*

In the 1750's, a method of printing a design on china instead of laboriously painting it by hand was invented in England. It is called *transfer-printing*: the design is engraved on copper, from which an impression is taken on a thin tissue paper, and thence transferred to the ware. This not only saves time but makes it possible to reproduce the same design exactly, over and over. Additional colors may be painted in by hand.

While these new and exciting developments in ceramics were going on in Europe, the majority of people, both there and in America, continued to use ordinary, inexpensive earthenware. Ceramics imported here came chiefly from England, and included a little soft-paste porcelain along with salt-glaze, delft, and variegated wares. The Continental porcelains, however, and many delightful types of Continental earthenware were unknown to most colonial Americans.

Developments in England

Several names stand out in connection with English ceramics during this period from the late 1600's to about 1775. Among them are the Elers brothers, who introduced redware to England; John Dwight, who contributed to the development of salt-glaze; John Astbury and his son Thomas, makers of salt-glaze, redware, variegated and other wares; Thomas Whieldon, who is credited with developing the colored glazes of variegated wares, and also naturalistic forms such as cauliflower and pineapple wares; Ralph Wood, all-round potter and modeler of earthenware figures; Thomas Fazackerley and Michael Edkins, decorators of delftware; John Sadler and Guy Green, pioneers in transfer-printing; William Duesbury of Chelsea, Bow, and Derby, and Dr. Wall of Worcester, makers of porcelain. But the most illustrious name of them all is that of Josiah Wedgwood, whose innovations in the late 1700's put an end to the making of salt-glaze and delftware and introduced a new period in ceramic history.

Today Wedgwood's name is most often associated with *jasperware* in its cameo-like designs, but that was

only one of his developments. Much more far-reaching in its effects was his perfection of *creamware,* a lead-glazed earthenware, light in weight, creamy in both color and texture. This led to the development of dinnerware as we know it today, complete matched sets for table use, in a pleasing, practical ware at a moderate price.

In 1763 Wedgwood obtained the patronage of Queen Charlotte for his creamware and christened it *Queen's ware.* The same type of thing, called

Wedgwood
Jasperware, 1790

simply creamware or cream-colored ware, was made by many English potters and imitated on the Continent.

It was used at first in shapes similar to those of contemporary silver, and often decorated with raised beading, molded edges, and pierced designs. Painting and transfer-printing were also frequent types of decoration. Piercing is often associated especially with Leeds, and black transfer-printed designs with Liverpool, but all these techniques were

Pierced Creamware, 1800

used on creamware by many potters in many places.

Among other types of ware that Wedgwood experimented with or perfected in the late 1700's and early 1800's were *basalt,* or black basaltes as it is sometimes called; *caneware,* a buff-colored stoneware; *rosso antico,* the old red stoneware with a new name; and *lusterware.*

While these were all types of earthenware or stoneware, an important new development in porcelain was made by another English potter, Josiah Spode. About 1800 he perfected the formula for *bone china.* Besides china clay and china stone, this contained considerable quantities of bone ash, which gave it its name. Bone china had many of the good qualities of both hard-paste and soft-paste porcelain, and was less expensive and less hazardous to produce than either. It met the demand for porcelain as a practical and not merely an ornamental ware, and proved so satisfactory that it has continued to be the material of fine dinnerware to this day.

Ceramics in the Nineteenth Century

By early Federal days in the United States, ceramics had come a long way in filling domestic needs. No longer was there a wide gap between the rather crude, utilitarian vessels in pottery and the elegant, scarce, and costly pieces in porcelain. The fine earthenwares approached porcelain in quality, and porcelain itself was no longer beyond reach.

As American trade developed after the Revolution, and particularly after the War of 1812, fine china was imported from France and Germany, export porcelain from China, and a variety of earthenwares from England. Creamware was available "plain and flowered," as it was advertised in the newspapers, or with other designs printed or painted. A particularly popular type was known as "edged," "blue edged," or "green edged"; it had a simple raised border touched with color.

English potters began catering consciously to the American market with such wares as Liverpool pitchers and Staffordshire dinner sets, transfer-printed with American historical views. Gaudy Dutch and spatterware, ironstone and mocha—a kind of creamware bordered with bands of color—were also imported here, as well as the varied wares that had been developed in the late 1700's.

From China, great amounts of the export porcelain, made to special order, were brought here. Complete dinner services consisting of hundreds of pieces poured into the seacoast towns. In every home that could afford it, the tea table and dining table were proudly set out with flowered or monogrammed pieces that are still the most prized of our early china.

Finally, American potters began competing with all this imported china. The American Pottery Manufacturing Company, established in Jersey City by the Hendersons in 1828, produced up-to-date wares comparable to some of the English, until 1845. After 1840 the pottery of Norton and Fenton at Bennington, Vermont, began the large production which made Bennington a household word. East Liverpool, Ohio, became a pottery-mak-

Transfer-Printed Earthenware, 1820's

Mocha Ware, 1810

ing center in the 1840's, making some porcelain as well as a good deal of heavy white "granite ware" or ironstone. Soon similar potteries operated in Indiana, New York, Pittsburgh, and Baltimore.

A stoneware pottery established in 1850 at Syracuse, New York, began making porcelain in 1888. A year later the Lenox china factory was set up at Trenton, New Jersey. Attempts at porcelain had been made with some success by Bonnin & Morris in Philadelphia as early as 1770, but the first major American production of porcelain was in the late 1820's and early 1830's. This was the work of William Ellis Tucker in Philadelphia. Most Tucker china is decorated with flowers and gilding, or painting in sepia, in imitation of French china of the time.

By the mid-1800's Americans were producing many kinds of useful and decorative wares. The making of ceramics, like the other old-time crafts, had been transformed into an industry.

Nevertheless, throughout the nineteenth century, most of the finer ceramic wares used here still came from abroad. There was porcelain from Meissen, Sèvres, and other Continental factories, Belleek porcelain from Ireland, and bone china and earthenware in great quantities from England. Among the most admired was Haviland, which was the proper bride's china for half a century. From about 1840 on, it was made in France expressly for the American market, at a factory established

Tucker China, 1830

Liverpool Jug, 1815

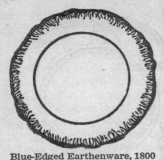

Blue-Edged Earthenware, 1800

by a New York importer named David Haviland. The factory was at Limoges, where pottery had been made since the late 1700's, and where other porcelain firms were presently located.

Meanwhile, likewise through the century, common earthenware and stoneware were made in many parts of the country, continuing the traditions of the 1600's and 1700's. Though we call them "common," they are often exceedingly attractive. Their simple shapes, pleasing colors, and bold designs appeal to many tastes far more than the delicacy or elaboration of porcelain.

The nineteenth-century wares are of vast variety. Some of them are hard to identify as to source, and even closely as to period, for many factories were competing with one another and consciously imitating each other's products.

Sprigged Ware, 1840

In the 1840's and later, the inexpensive English wares included the printed Staffordshire, ironstone, parian, the sprigged ware that is miscalled "Chelsea," and molded wares in octagonal and paneled shapes that reflected the contemporary Gothic taste. "Apostle" pitchers belong to this period. So do the brown, hound-handled pitchers.

Hound-Handled Pitcher, 1850

More elegant wares became more ornate. There was a fondness for elaborately painted and gilded porcelain. In shapes and decoration one can trace the prevailing trend through the classic of the Greek Revival, the neo-Gothic, the neo-rococo, and the romantic styles of the 1800's. China was much used for vases, large ornamental urns, and lamps. Tableware became more plentiful and varied than ever before, and new forms appeared.

Rockingham Porcelain, 1830

The fashion for figures which developed in the 1700's was not limited to that period, but the figures most highly prized today are those of the eighteenth century. These are hard-paste porcelain from Meissen and other German factories; soft-paste from Chelsea, Bow, and Derby in England, Chantilly and Sèvres in France; and the English figures in pottery.

There are also figures, usually of birds and animals, in Pennsylvania pottery of the late 1700's and the 1800's. Though crude in comparison with porcelain figures, they are often boldly modeled, colorful, and lively.

Through the 1800's Staffordshire produced many gaily colored small "cottage figures" in earthenware, and the almost life-size Staffordshire dogs with tawny hair. Bennington made its parian figures and brown-glazed animals in the mid-1800's.

Recently there has been a vogue for so-called bisque figures. *Bisque* is the French word for *biscuit,* which is porcelain or earthenware that has been fired but not glazed. Bisque figures were made at various porcelain factories in the 1700's, but those popular today are mostly French and date from the late 1800's. Usually sentimental representations of children, colored in pastel shades, they lack the artistry of the early figures.

English Porcelain, 1840

Many of those early figures have been reproduced, in the

Derby Porcelain,
1810

nineteenth century and up to the present. Meissen, for instance, repeated many of its early models a century after they had first appeared, even shaping them in the original molds. Meissen figures have also been imitated by many other potters. Later copies, however, rarely if ever recapture the delicacy of modeling and coloring of the originals.

These are only a few of the more familiar types of ceramic figures. Clay is a plastic material, and potters have always modeled it into pleasing ornaments.

Marks on Ceramics

Potters have often marked their wares, and their marks are of many kinds, from a cryptic symbol to a complete name and address, with even a trade name for the pattern of the piece. Such marks as the latter usually date after 1825. Marks may be scratched, impressed, painted, or printed. Sometimes they are on the bottom of a piece, sometimes on a quite conspicuous part of the surface.

A convenient guide to these marks is *Handbook of Old Pottery and Porcelain Marks* by C. Jordan Thorn (New York, 1947).

Many desirable examples of early china are quite unmarked, however, and marks should not be relied on solely for identification. They have been too often imitated, a practice not

Porcelain
Ewer, 1860

limited to the unscrupulous today. Several potteries in the 1700's, for instance, used a mark very like the famous crossed swords of Meissen. Moreover, a modern mark applied in all good faith by a modern manufacturer can be scraped off and the piece represented as old. Besides the mark, the character of body, glaze, modeling, and decoration must all be taken into consideration in identifying ceramics.

Sèvres
Porcelain, 1805

Notes on Some Familiar Wares and Their Makers

Chinese export porcelain is the generic name for the ware made in great quantities in China in the 1700's and 1800's for export to Europe and America. It was decorated to special order, after designs sent out from the Occident, and is not representative of Chinese work made for the Chinese. Some made for the European market was painted with coats of arms of royalty or nobility and was extremely rich in decoration.

American-market pieces, hand painted in several colors, have patriotic designs such as eagles; armorial or pseudo-armorial devices, monograms, and ciphers; ships, Biblical scenes, floral designs, and pictures copied from engravings. Certain armorial and presentation pieces are the most highly prized by collectors.

This ware was made in complete tea and dinner services, punchbowls, pitchers, mugs, and flagons, mantel garnitures, and various other forms. Often the shapes are modeled after contemporary silver forms. A few of the most typical are illustrated here.

The ware is a hard-paste porcelain, a rather cold white or a bit grayish in color. Sometimes the glaze is rather pebbly; this is called an *orange-peel glaze*.

After the Revolution when American trade with China began, this porcelain was a major import and great quantities were brought here. Originally the trade in it had been carried on by the East India Companies of England and the Continent, and for that reason it was called *East India china*.

In the latter 1800's a mistaken notion became spread about that this ware had been made not in China but in a little seacoast town of England named Lowestoft, and

Chinese Export Porcelain, 1790

the porcelain came to be known almost everywhere as *Lowestoft* or *Oriental Lowestoft*. This was an unfortunate misnomer that has been hard to correct. The china is still very widely called Lowestoft, but the accepted names for it are *Chinese export porcelain* or—more popular today—China Trade porcelain.

There was actually some porcelain made in the town of Lowestoft, but it is not common, and is quite easy to distinguish from the export porcelain. It is soft-paste, and its decoration, usually in blue and red, is most often simple floral designs, not too finely painted.

The Oriental export porcelain with its armorial and other designs in various colors was shipped from the

port of Canton, though it was made some three hundred miles inland at the great pottery center of Ch'ing-te-chen. The name *Canton* ware, however, is reserved for a certain type of blue-and-white porcelain, which was made at potteries near Canton as well as at Ch'ing-te-chen. This

Canton Porcelain, 1820

was tremendously popular with the American market and was imported in quantities from 1785 on.

Canton ware was made in complete dinner and tea services and many specialized table forms. Its decoration was a native Chinese design, not something ordered by the purchaser. It consisted of a scene of islands, boats, bridges, and trees, painted under the glaze in blue. This is the ancestor of the *willow pattern* in all its variations, which is discussed below under the heading *Staffordshire*.

The name *Nanking* is also applied to wares of this type, and sometimes the two names are used interchangeably, though a distinction can be made between them. Nanking is a smoother, finer porcelain, has a more elaborate border, and is better painted, often with gilding added. After 1830 both types deteriorated in quality but they continued in popularity through a good part of the 1800's and have indeed been made and imported to the present day.

Dresden. The oldest and most famous of the porcelain factories is in some ways the most confusing. The factory was, and is, actually located in the town of Meissen, in Saxony, Germany. This is only a few miles from the capital town of Dresden. At Dresden was located the court of Augustus the Strong, Elector of Saxony and founder of the factory. That is why in the 1700's and ever since, Meissen porcelain has been called Dresden porcelain.

The first of the famous names associated with Meissen is Johann Friedrich Boettger, who discovered the secret of making hard-paste porcelain. He worked at Meissen from the founding of the factory in 1710 till his death in 1719.

Johann G. Herold was the outstanding painter of early Meissen. He worked at the factory for many years, from 1720 on.

Johann Kaendler was the greatest Meissen modeler. He came to the factory in 1731 and remained until his death in 1775. He modeled many figures, and his influence was a major factor in Meissen's success.

The early years, from 1720 to about 1760, were the great years of Meissen, when the wares were produced that are most highly prized today.

The "Marcolini period" was from 1774 to 1814, when Count Marcolini was director of the works. Pieces made during that period are in the neo-classic style.

During the nineteenth century Meissen did little in the way of originating new wares or new designs. Much of what it produced was in reproduction of its eighteenth-century models.

Gaudy Dutch, gaudy Welsh, or just *gaudyware* are names given to a certain type of English earthenware with gay, colorful floral designs. For many years it was believed that this ware was made in Pennsylvania because it was mostly found there—hence the name Dutch. Actually it was made in Staffordshire. Its greatest period of popularity was from about 1815 to 1830, but similar inexpensive "cottage wares" were made throughout the 1800's.

Gaudyware originated as an inexpensive imitation of

brightly painted porcelains with Imari designs, produced in the early 1800's by Derby, Worcester, and others. Favorite designs in gaudyware are king's rose, war bonnet, and butterfly. The painted red, blue, and yellow decoration is applied over the glaze, and sometimes portions of the design have been previously transfer-printed or painted under the glaze in blue.

Gaudyware, 1820

Ironstone is a heavy white china that has been produced since the early 1800's. The potter particularly associated with it is James Mason of Staffordshire, who patented his "process for the improvement of the manufacture of English porcelain" in 1814. The ware has been made ever since, by many other potters as well as the Mason firm. In America it has been made since the 1860's. It has been called *stone china, opaque china,* and *white granite,* among other names. As these names imply, it is a strong, utilitarian ware.

A great deal of ironstone is undecorated, and is often seen in the rather angular shapes of the 1840's to 1870's. Some of the earlier ware was painted in floral designs, some in imitation of Chinese porcelain. A more typical kind of decoration was transfer printing in colors.

Luster, or more properly *lusterware,* is the name given to china decorated with shiny, metallic colors called lusters. English lusterware, made from about 1800 on, is of three main kinds—silver, copper, and gold.

Silver luster is made from platinum, not from silver. The first pieces were an attempt to simulate real silver. The shapes followed silver forms, and were entirely coated with the metallic silver pigment.

More familiar is *silver resist,* made chiefly between 1805 and 1815. This was produced by covering with a resinous substance, which would resist the luster, all the surface except the pattern; then applying the luster all over, and finally washing off the resin. The design in silver luster then stood out against the plain background.

Copper luster, made from copper, was also used occasionally to cover a piece completely, but more often was combined with some other type of decoration, such as embossed designs. Transfer-printed designs were used with both copper and silver luster. Copper luster is the commonest of the three kinds, especially after 1820.

Gold luster, made from gold, produced all the shades ranging from orange and pink to purple. Some fine effects in delicate mottled shades were produced about 1800 by Wedgwood and others. Pitchers, mugs, and some other forms with pinkish splotches of luster, combined with transfer-printed designs, were made at Sunderland between 1815 and 1840. Painted decoration was often combined with pink (gold) luster. In the 1820's and 1830's luster of this color was frequently confined to

Copper Luster, 1825

a rim or band or a decorative spattering of floral motifs.

Majolica is one of the late wares collected now. It is earthenware molded in naturalistic shapes and decorated with glazes in various colors. It was made in England from the early 1800's on but most of what is found dates after our Civil War. In America it was made especially by Griffen, Smith & Hill at Phoenixville, Pennsylvania, in the 1880's. They called their ware *Etruscan majolica.* It imitated the old Whieldon-type wares in having colored glazes and cauliflower shapes, but is usually more complicated in shape and less rich in coloring. The seaweed and shell is another very familiar pattern. This nineteenth-century majolica should not be confused with the Spanish and Italian lusterwares of two and three centuries earlier which are called *maiolica.* The two types are similar in name but not in character or in looks.

Majolica, 1880

Parian ware, 1855

Parian ware was developed in the 1840's by Copeland (Spode works) of Staffordshire, and became very popular for ornamental figures as well as modeled vases and tablewares. It was named for Parian marble, but contrary to popular belief it is not made of marble. It is an unglazed porcelain, very well adapted to figure modeling. In fact, quite colossal figures and ornamental objects were made of it in the 1850's. Parian ware was produced not only by its originator but also by Minton and numerous other English potters. In America it was made at Bennington, where parian pitchers and vases often had floral patterns.

Rockingham. In 1826 a pottery at Swinton in Yorkshire took the name of the Marquis of Rockingham. It operated until 1842, making porcelain with rather elaborate floral decoration.

The name Rockingham, or more properly *Rockingham glaze,* is applied to much ware that did not come from this factory, however. It refers to a mottled lead glaze in shades of brown and buff which was used on earthenwares, not porcelain. Such wares were in fact produced at Swinton in the late 1700's, before it became the Rockingham works, but in the 1800's a similar molasses-like glaze was made at many other places. It is seen on hound-handled and apostle pitchers, on pudding molds, and on a quantity of household forms. Nowadays, *Rockingham* is used commercially as a general term for common earthenware.

A similar glaze but with added streaks of green and blue was used on buff clay at Bennington to make *flint-enamel ware*. It was patented by Fenton in 1849.

Spatterware, also called *spongeware,* is a whitish earthenware which takes its name from its decoration: a wide border, or sometimes almost all the surface, is covered with a stippling in blue, red, or green, spattered on with a sponge. Usually there is a design in the center—a peacock, eagle, flower, or house—hand-painted with simplicity and naiveté. Spatterware was made before 1800 but most of what is found today is of about 1825 to 1840.

It was produced in Staffordshire, largely for the American market.

Staffordshire is a county in England where pottery has been made since Roman times. The name does not identify any single type of ware, because Staffordshire has produced almost all the kinds that have been made in England: slip-decorated, salt-glaze, redware, Whieldon-type, variegated earthenwares, creamware, jasper, bone china, luster, and the rest. Today it is still the center of England's ceramic industry, where Spode, Wedgwood, Minton, Doulton, Ridgway, and other well-known firms are located.

The name "Staffordshire china," however, commonly refers to the *transfer-printed* wares of the 1800's, especially those with American-historical views. The earliest transfer-printed designs, from about 1755 on, had been in black or red or blue, sometimes with additional colors painted in by hand. They were used on tiles, mugs, pitchers, and tea things.

After 1800 the advantages of transfer-printing for complete sets of matching tableware were exploited. Designs were printed in a strong deep blue, the familiar color of our "old blue," and after the War of 1812 many were created especially to appeal to the American market. Their decoration consists of American scenes, portraits, and patriotic emblems.

After about 1830 such all-over designs were printed in many other colors—pink, light blue, sepia, mulberry, green—singly or in combination. Romantic scenes and fanciful designs gradually became more popular than the historical ones.

The leading Staffordshire makers of these wares for the American market were Adams, Clews, Jackson, Ridgway, Stevenson, Stubbs, Enoch Wood. Transfer-printing on earthenware has been done by many others, however, in Staffordshire and elsewhere, from the 1700's to the present.

The best-known and best-loved of all the transfer-printed designs is the *willow pattern*. This was originally an adaptation of a Chinese design called the island or rivers pattern, which was used on blue-and-white porcelain imported to Europe in the 1700's. Its first use in

England was about 1780, when it was produced by Thomas Turner at Staffordshire. The design was engraved by Thomas Minton, at that time an apprentice to Turner and later founder of the Minton pottery that still operates. The design was copied and adapted by many other potters, and Minton himself engraved many variants of it.

By 1800 the willow pattern was pretty much common property among potters. Between 1800 and 1830 it was used on both earthenware and porcelain by every significant pottery in England as well as by many in France and Germany. It has been produced continuously up to this day, and one of the ironies of the industrial era is that china for the Woolworth market was made in Japan in imitation of the English imitation of the Chinese design.

The willow pattern is so popular that everyone recognizes its river with the bridge across it and plumed trees along the bank, and everyone knows the legend that the two birds above are the souls of two lovers fleeing from an angry father.

4. Glass

The kinds of glass most widely collected in this country today are the pressed tablewares in matching patterns and sets, and the art glass in ornamental forms and colors. Both of these are less than a hundred years old, while the craft of glassmaking goes back literally for thousands of years.

The ancient Mediterranean civilization knew all the essential techniques of fashioning and decorating glass that are known today, except mechanical pressing. Centuries later the same techniques were rediscovered and practiced throughout Europe, and finally they were brought to America.

Glassmaking in America began with the first English colony settled at Jamestown in 1607. No glass survives, however, which is positively known to have been made at Jamestown or at one of the few other glasshouses established here in the 1600's; and little American glass of the 1700's exists today.

The great bulk of what is known and collected as "early American" glass was made after 1800, and much of it after 1850. Thus it is really late in terms of American history, and extremely so in terms of glassmaking history.

It was not until the 1800's that glass came into fairly general use here except for windows and bottles. Drinking vessels, pitchers, bowls for many uses, and a few other utensils had been available in domestic and imported glass, but to a limited extent. Inexpensive pottery, pewter, or wood filled the needs of most people until the nineteenth century's increased production and lowered costs put glass within easier financial reach.

In glass it is much harder to trace a logical progression of styles than, for instance, in furniture. Forms and fashions changed, of course, and certain characteristics distinguish the products of one era or one region from another, but early techniques and forms persisted side by side with new developments. To fix dates and sources of glass, it is therefore important to study the character of the glass itself.

Glassmaking Techniques

The basic materials of glass are silica (usually sand) and alkalis. These are mixed to form the *batch,* which is melted to produce the molten glass called the *metal.*

Blown Glass Pitcher

Practically all glass made before about 1825 was blown by human lung power. In this process, which is still practiced, a *gather* of the metal is blown into a bubble on a *blowpipe* and held, while being worked, on a *pontil* or *punty rod;* and is manipulated with various tools including *pucellas, tongs,* and *shears.* It is then slowly cooled or *annealed* in the annealing oven or *leer.*

When the piece is broken off from the pontil rod, a rough spot called a *pontil mark* is left. On old glass this was sometimes polished away, as it usually is today; thus a pontil mark is not in itself an indication of date.

The *bull's eye* in glass panes sometimes seen as transom or side lights around old doorways is actually the pontil scar at the center of a sheet of crown window glass.

Glass formed by blowing and manipulation alone is called *offhand blown* or *freeblown.* Glass can also be blown into a mold, to give it shape or pattern. When blown into an open-top *dip mold* or part-size *piece mold,*

Pattern-Molded
Sugar Bowl

Blown-Three-Mold Pitcher

then removed and expanded by further blowing, it is called *pattern-molded* or *blown-molded*. Patterns thus formed are ribs or swirls, diamonds, or other simple geometric motifs.

Glass can also be blown into a full-size mold. This process, though known in ancient glass, was chiefly practiced in America in the 1820's and 1830's to produce an inexpensive imitation of cut glass. It is called *blown-three-mold* glass, because the molds were customarily in three pieces, though two- and four-part ones were also used. Seam marks left by the joints of the mold can usually be detected. The patterns have been classified as geometric, arch, and baroque.

Sometimes early glass was ornamented in relief by means of blobs or threads of molten glass applied or trailed over the surface and tooled into a desired shape. This produced the leaf-like swirl called *lilypad,* and also *threading. Crimping* and *rigaree,* which gave a crumpled ribbon effect, and *prunts,* or small shaped knobs, were also produced by tooling. Streaks of colored or opaque glass were worked into the clear metal in *loopings* and *swirls.*

Engraved Decanter

A widely used form of decoration was *engraving*. This was usually accomplished with a copper wheel, more rarely with a diamond point which gave a more delicate effect. Engraving should not be confused with *etching*, achieved by use of acid, and having a frosted, less sculptural appearance. Commercial etching of glass dates from the late 1800's but engraving is an ancient process.

Lilypad Pitcher with Threaded Neck

Cutting is an old technique that gives particular brilliance to glass by converting the smooth rounded surface into a pattern of contrasting planes that reflect the light. The all-over, sparkling designs deeply and sharply cut in thick, heavy glass date from the 1880's into the 1900's. Early cutting was at first broader and simpler in de-

Cut-Glass Pitcher

sign and more sparsely used than that late type, and even when more complicated patterns were developed it was shallower and less sharply cut than that of the end of the century.

Still another kind of early decoration was *enameling*, painting a design on the surface in colors which became fused with the glass by heating. *Gilding* sometimes accompanied enameling, sometimes was used without it.

European Glass

As practiced in Europe these fundamental techniques developed two or three main glassmaking traditions that were to influence the craft in America. *Venetian glass,* which reached its peak in the 1400's, is noted for its delicacy, thinness, fragility, and frilly applied ornamentation. *German glass* became famous in the 1600's for its balanced forms, enameled and gilded decoration, cutting, and exquisite engraving. There was also a quantity of cruder glass, green and fairly thick, produced by outlying houses in Germany and called "forest glass" or peasant glass. Spain, France, and the Netherlands

Enameled Flip Glass

developed their own characteristics, but the other glassmaking region of particular interest to Americans is England, because of its close relation to glassmaking here.

In early *English glass,* both Venetian and German influences are apparent, but by the eighteenth century England too had developed types distinctively her own. English glass of this period happily combined features of both Venetian and Ger-

man, but with less fragility than the one and more simplicity than the other.

England also contributed a new ingredient to glass,
lead, which made it clearer and easier to manipulate
and decorate. Invention of *lead glass,* also called *flint
glass,* is credited to the English glassmaker George Ra-
venscroft, about 1675. It is differentiated from *non-lead
glass,* in which soda and often lime are the chief alkalis.
Lead glass is more brilliant and generally considered
of finer quality than non-lead. You cannot tell one from
the other however, merely by their appearance. Tests for
detecting the presence of lead are applied by specialists.

London, Bristol, Newcastle, and Stourbridge were
making glass in the 1600's. Up to about 1780 they all
produced glass in the successive types and styles that are
grouped together as English glass.

Bristol distinguished itself by its enameled opaque-
white but made other contemporary types as well, and
continued to make glass into the 1870's. Before that time
Birmingham had become a center for the industry, and
also Nailsea where the first factory was established in
1788.

The name Nailsea is especially associated with glass
in two or three colors, usually including opaque white,
which has a mottled, looped, swirled, or striped effect,
though such wares were also made at Newcastle and elsewhere. Nailsea continued them until the works closed
in 1873.

Yorkshire and Tyneside became centers of cut and
pressed glassmaking in the early 1800's. Ornamental and
table wares in the taste of the period were made at London, Birmingham, and elsewhere to the end of the century. After 1860 Stourbridge became the source of the
finest English glass, finest in metal and in design, and
it remains today the center of the British industry for
better-quality table and ornamental wares.

From England glassmaking spread to Ireland. The
great period of glassmaking in Ireland began in 1780
when the achievement of free trade there coincided with
new heavy taxes on glass in England, causing English
manufacturers to move their operations to Ireland. The

period continued till about 1825, when an Irish excise tax made glassmaking unprofitable in Ireland. During that time it was English influence and English glass-making traditions that were expressed in glass made, largely by Englishmen, in Ireland. Thus while Irish glass is a recognizable type, it is really a continuation of English glassmaking rather than a native development.

Irish Cut-Glass Bowl

The type is clear cut glass in simple shapes, such forms as oval or round footed bowls, globular or urn-shaped sugar bowls and jars, drinking vessels, candlesticks and candelabra with faceted pendants. The cutting is relatively shallow, simple, and broad in scale as compared with the brilliant, deep faceting of the late 1800's. Its designs are usually swags, lozenge shapes, diamonds, sunbursts, and horizontal prisms. Edges of bowls are frequently cut in scallops or points.

The leading Irish glasshouses were at Waterford, Belfast, Dublin, and Cork, where both the Cork Glass Company and the Waterloo Company operated. Rarely the factory's name is molded in the base of decanters or other objects. There is a popular but unfounded belief that you can always recognize Waterford glass by its grayish tone; while some Waterford glass has this tinge, the factory actually achieved a quite colorless clear metal.

Some colored glass was also made at the Irish factories, and pattern-molded, blown-three-mold, and engraved glass was made besides cut glass, but the cut glass is considered typical and was probably their finest product. All these factories had gone out of business by the 1870's, and their great contribution ended soon after 1825.

Because of the relationship between Irish and English glass between 1780 and 1825, it is often impossible to tell in which country a given piece was made.

American Blown Glass

The European traditions were brought to America, both in actual glass and in the minds and hands of glassmakers. Although limited quantities of glass were imported to America from earliest days, glass for table use remained relatively rare until the time of the Revolution. Between then and the mid-1800's English and Irish glass was brought here in increasing quantities—wineglasses and decanters particularly, bowls and ornamental forms, candlesticks and even chandeliers. Before 1800 French glass was also being imported, and its quantities increased throughout the nineteenth century. In the second half of the 1800's, Bohemian glass in table and ornamental forms became extremely popular.

Of the numerous glasshouses built in America before the Revolution, two are important for their contribution to our glassmaking history—Caspar Wistar's, established in southern New Jersey in 1739; and Henry William Stiegel's, begun at Manheim, Pennsylvania, in 1769.

The workmen at the South Jersey factory came from the Continent and followed the German tradition in which they had been trained. Therefore the name *South Jersey-type* is applied to a certain kind of American glass which reflects that German tradition. The type is free-blown, fairly thick, ornamented with threading, lilypads, prunts, loopings, and the like. The most frequent items are pitchers, bowls, and pans.

Stiegel's workmen came from both England and the Continent, and brought influences from both to establish what we call our Stiegel tradition. Glass of *Stiegel-type* includes both free-blown and blown-molded, clear and colored, engraved and enameled, in a variety of pieces for table and ornamental use.

One other glasshouse founded here before 1800 left its mark, that of John Frederick Amelung in Maryland. Its engraved glass in the German tradition was the first American glass that could compare with the better European wares, though it could not rival the best. It is free-blown in table and ornamental forms, often engraved with distinctive leaf and flower motifs, garlands, initials, or ciphers. Most of it is clear, characterized by a grayish color of metal, though a few amethyst pieces are known.

Though Wistar's and Stiegel's glass ventures had ceased before the Revolution and Amelung's before 1800, their traditions continued well into the nineteenth century. South Jersey-type glass was made in New England, New York, Pennsylvania, and Ohio, as well as in New Jersey, even in the late 1800's. Stiegel-type traveled westward through Maryland and Pennsylvania into Ohio, where it persisted equally long. Workmen from Amelung's factory also moved west to produce similar glass in new glassmaking ventures. While these free-blown and mold-blown types were made in many parts of the country, after 1800 production of the more sophisticated engraved and cut types became centered around Pittsburgh and the seaboard cities of the east.

American Pressed Glass

About 1825 manufacturers in this country began fashioning glass by a new process—the first innovation in glassmaking techniques since ancient days. This was mechanical pressing: the metal was forced into a mold by a mechanically driven plunger instead of by blowing. This new invention virtually revolutionized the glassmaking industry, because it introduced mass production and made possible a great variety of new wares at lowered costs. For the first time people could buy entire sets of glass tableware in matching forms and patterns, at moderate prices.

The earlier products of the pressing machine were what we call *lacy* or *lace* glass. Though the glass itself is fairly thick, the designs are intricate and rather delicate; the backgrounds are finely stippled with tiny raised dots, giving them bril-

Lacy Glass Plate

liance and a truly lacy effect, for which they are named.

Toward the mid-century this type began to be superseded by *pattern glass,* without the stippled background. Matching tableware was produced in hundreds of different patterns, from the relatively simple and early *Ashburton, horn-of-plenty,* and *bellflower* to such elaborate and often coarse products of the 1880's as *daisy and button* and *shell and tassel.* It was made at Sandwich and other New England factories, in New York, New Jersey, and Philadelphia, and also throughout the midwestern glassmaking area of which Pittsburgh was the center.

The interest in collecting nineteenth-century pattern glass has increased tremendously in the past twenty years, and prices have gone up accordingly. Many people like to use it on their tables, and one of its fascinations for collectors is the possibility of finding matching pieces to complete a set.

Colored Glass

Both lead and non-lead glass were made in America before 1800. Normally non-lead glass is *green glass,* more or less strongly tinted in shades of dull or pale green, aquamarine, brownish, and yellowish. This was the common early window and bottle glass. This tinge of color could be removed and the glass made clear or colorless by the addition of black oxide of manganese to the batch. A kind of non-lead glass called *lime glass,* much used after the Civil War for pressed and other inexpensive wares, was as clear as lead glass but cheaper.

Crystal is a name sometimes used to mean clear or uncolored glass, though sometimes reserved for clear blown glass of fine quality and exceptional purity. In modern usage it has become a generic term for blown-glass tableware. Strictly, the name refers to *rock crystal,* a natural colorless mineral which glass sought to resemble.

Aside from green glass, which is glass in its "natural" color, colored glass in countless hues and tones is achieved artificially by addition of certain chemicals, usually metallic oxides, to the batch. Glass in colors has been made from earliest days.

In early American blown wares, some rich blues,

greens, and amethysts occur, in addition to the attractive shades of aquamarine, soft green, and amber. Opaque or milk glass and opalescent glass also were made early in Europe, but here they are found chiefly in the pressed wares after 1825, which also occur in a greater variety of other shades and colors than had been made previously.

Old glass sometimes undergoes deterioration which produces an almost crackled appearance called *crizzling.* This was most common in the early attempts to produce lead glass. Non-lead glass also sometimes develops a cloudy appearance, due probably to impurities in the metal, and is called *sick glass.* It has sometimes been "cured" by chemical treatment.

Somewhat before the mid-1800's American glassmakers also began making what is called *cased* or *overlay* glass adopting a technique that had been practiced earlier in Europe. The type is associated especially with Bohemia, which produced so much of it that *Bohemian* glass came to be a generic name for it, no matter where it was made. This glass consists of a core of glass encased within a thin coating or layer of glass of another color, or several coatings of different colors. Such glass may be decorated by cutting a design through the outer layer or layers to reveal the clear or colored glass beneath. Though technically cased glass and overlay are the same thing, the name overlay usually refers to glass decorated in this way, and cased is reserved for glass whose outer layer is not cut.

Overlay Pitcher

Art Glass

Along about 1880 glass manufacturers added several new strings to their bow in the form of what are called *fancy wares* or *art glass.* Experimentation in glassmaking resulted in new techniques for producing ornamental effects in color and finish, and a whole crop of new wares, often with names even fancier than the glass, appeared on the market. The distinctive character of most of them depends on their color and texture. Recent though they are, they are widely collected today. The more familiar of these variegated wares are identified by their respective trade names under the heading *Types of Art Glass* at the end of this chapter.

Novelties in Glass

There are a great many minor forms in American glass that can be classed as novelties, such small objects as glass hats, shoes, slippers, canes, rolling pins, witch balls, animals. Some of them are blown glass in the South Jersey tradition and were made fairly early in the 1800's. Such are the varicolored canes and rolling pins, and the so-called witch balls which are hollow spheres of glass, often colored and with white loopings. Their name goes back, no doubt, to some now-forgotten superstition or legend; actually they were often placed in the flaring mouth of a pitcher to serve as a cover. Hats and shoes are sometimes freeblown, sometimes partially patterned in a mold intended for a tumbler or inkwell.

Novelties in Glass

Such novelties or whimsies are sometimes called end-of-the-day pieces, and it is believed that they were made by glassblowers in their free time, out of unused metal left over at the end of the day. Many of the pitchers, bowls, and table forms in South Jersey-type glass were also made in this way and not intended for commercial use.

In the latter half of the 1800's novelty forms were commercially produced in quantity, and pressed as often as free blown. Besides an astonishing variety of hats, shoes, and boots, there are covered dishes with lids in the form of barnyard fowl and dogs or other animals, matchboxes and toothpick holders, cornucopias, dishes in the form of hands, miniatures of household objects, baskets, and more other forms than one could list. Some are charming, some amusing, and some merely grotesque.

Reproductions

Many of the pressed-glass patterns have been reproduced and the copies are often very misleading. Some of the early American blown-glass types have also been reproduced, and some modern Mexican glass is so like the early American that it can be mistaken for it.

You have probably seen someone strike the edge of a piece of glass and say with a knowing smile, "Ah, that's Sandwich. You can tell by the ring." Actually, you can't. A brand-new piece of Steuben glass will give off just as fine a ring, and some Sandwich glass will sound quite dead. Any glass made of good-quality metal will ring, especially when it is blown and quite thin, and in a simple round form.

There is no easy, infallible rule for telling old glass from new. As with any other kind of antiques, it takes knowledge and experience.

American Glassmakers

Of the hundreds of glass factories that have operated in America since 1607, a few stand out because they were really significant in the development of American glassmaking, or because the glass they made happens to appeal particularly to collectors. Some of the most familiar names of men, factories, and glassmaking centers are given here, with a few highlights of their history.

John Frederick Amelung, a native of Bremen, Germany, operated his glassworks at New Bremen, Frederick County, Maryland, from 1787 to 1795. Amelung glass is rare, but important for its quality and its influence on later glassmaking efforts. It is mostly clear, and engraved in a characteristic manner. Several presentation pieces, with engraved inscriptions, are in museums and private collections, and serve as key pieces for identifying others.

Cambridge is the name by which the New England Glass Company of Cambridge, Massachusetts, is usually known. The factory operated from 1818 to 1888. Its products were of first quality, and included virtually every kind of glass being made in this country during that long time. Deming Jarves was agent of the company before founding the Sandwich works.

Ohio was an active part of what is called the midwestern glassmaking area from 1815 until the 1860's. Factories at Zanesville, Mantua, and Kent are the best known. They produced freeblown and pattern-molded glass. The midwestern area also included Wheeling and other centers in what is now West Virginia, and the region around Pittsburgh and western Pennsylvania.

Pittsburgh was the pioneer in the midwestern glassmaking area, and remained the leader in quantity and quality of production. The first works there was established in 1797 by O'Hara and Craig. In 1808 the company was founded that was to be Bakewell and Company, Bakewell and Page, then Bakewell, Page and Bakewell, and finally Bakewell, Pears, and Company, before it went out of business in 1882. This firm, the first in America to be successful at making cut glass commercially, also made practically every other type of glassware popular in its time. A kind of pattern molding called *pillar molding,* which formed thick vertical or swirled ridges on the surface of a piece of glass, is especially associated with Pittsburgh.

Sandwich is one of the best-known names in American glass. In 1825 Deming Jarves founded a glass factory at Sandwich, Massachusetts, of which the proper name was originally the Sandwich Manufacturing Company and soon became the Boston & Sandwich Glass Company. Jarves was general manager of the firm till 1858, when he resigned to set up the Cape Cod Glass Company nearby. The Sandwich works continued in business till 1888 as one of the leading glassworks in the country. The first pressing of glass in the late 1820's is usually, if wrongly, credited to Sandwich, and pressed glass was a great part of its output. However, though the name Sandwich is often carelessly used as a synonym for pressed glass, it was only one of many factories producing it, and pressed glass was only one of its varied products. These also included blown-three-mold and some blown, cut, and engraved glass in the factory's early days, and later much overlay, art glass of various kinds, paperweights, and blown decorative wares. (See also *Types of Art Glass, Striped.*)

William Henry Stiegel was a colorful character who liked to live flamboyantly and be called the Baron, was jailed for debt, and died in poverty. Born in Cologne, Germany, in 1729, he came to America in 1750; from 1752 to 1763 ran an iron furnace in Pennsylvania; and from 1763 to 1774 was producing the glass that has made him a legend. He had three glasshouses, one at Elizabeth Furnace, two at Manheim, Pennsylvania. Glass collectors used to call all early pattern-molded, enameled, and engraved glass Stiegel, just as they called all pressed glass Sandwich. Now we know that little of it can positively be ascribed to him; similar types were made in Germany and England, and later in other American factories.

Caspar Wistar was not the first glassmaker in America, but he was the first successful one. He was a German, born in 1696, who came to America in 1717, settling in Philadelphia. In 1739 he built a glassworks in Salem County, New Jersey, which he ran until 1752. Then his son Richard took over and continued until about 1780. We know from records that the Wistar factory made window glass and bottles of various kinds, and believe its glass represented what we now call South Jersey type. No actual example of this type, however, has been positively ascribed to it.

Many other American glassmakers have been recorded, and probably still others once existed which have now been quite forgotten. While a few factories operated successfully over a long period of time, many were short-lived, ill-fated ventures—experiments that failed. A geographical listing of the known American glassmakers from 1608 to the present is included, along with a vast amount of information on what they made, in the very comprehensive book, *American Glass,* by George S. and Helen McKearin (New York, 1941).

Bottles and Flasks

A major product of most early glasshouses in America was bottles, and most of the bottles were for wine and spirits. Up to 1800 these were more squat and bulbous than liquor bottles of today. Besides large bottles there were small pocket flasks of various kinds, and also bottles for snuff, bitters, medicines, perfume.

Some bottles and flasks were produced in the glass of Stiegel type. These were pattern-molded in designs of ribs or diamonds or the rare *diamond-daisy* or *daisy-in-square*. They are rather bulbous and oval or egg-shaped, less often almost globular. The principal colors are greens, blues, and amethyst. While this type was made by Stiegel, it was also produced elsewhere in this country and in Europe.

Blown Glass
Pocket Flask

Another eighteenth-century small flask, which continued into the 1800's, is the Pitkin type; it is pattern-molded with ribbing, vertical or swirled. It was made by the "half-post" method which involved a second dipping in the metal and gave an extra thickness of glass around the body; the edge of the second layer is clearly visible at the base of the neck. Pitkin flasks are usually fatter than Stiegel-type, and occur most often in shades of dull green or amber. Pattern-molded flasks in the Stiegel tradition were produced in Ohio and the mid-western glassmaking area in the early 1800's. So also was a distinctive type of long-necked, bulbous or globular bottle, pattern-molded. Colors are most often soft greens and ambers.

Pattern-Molded
Bottle,
Midwestern

Huge, globular, blown-glass bottles with small necks, of gallon capacity or more, are called *carboys*. They were used for shipping beverages or chemicals and are often not so old as their crude greenish glass might suggest. Many date late in the 1800's.

The most varied and to many people the most interesting of nineteenth-century bottles are the pictorial and
historical flasks. They were made from the 1820's until
late in the century, by many American glasshouses. Designed as whiskey bottles, they are of half-pint and pint
capacity, and after about 1850 of quart capacity as well.
Their colors are most frequently shades of soft green,
amber, and aquamarine, but rich greens, blues, yellows,
and rarely amethyst also occur. They were made by blowing in full-size, two-piece molds which have the pictorial
decoration that imparts their chief interest. For these
designs are to glass what Currier & Ives prints are to pictures; they are virtually a record of historical, social, and
economic events through the period of their production.

The most numerous up to 1850 are portrait flasks, and
the people whose faces are memorialized in this way included presidents like Washington, Adams, Jackson; mil-
itary heroes like Lafayette, Ringgold, Kossuth; statesmen
like Clay and Franklin; notables like Jenny Lind and De
Witt Clinton. There are besides many patriotic designs
based on eagles, Columbia, and the American flag;
Masonic emblems; railroad designs; naval designs with
pictures of ships; and designs commemorating or carica-
turing some contemporary event, such as the *Union* flasks
of Civil War times, and the *Pike's Peak* flasks associated
with the Colorado gold rush.

And finally there is a large group of flasks with conventional designs—sunbursts, cornucopias, and the scroll
used on items called, because of their shape, *violin* flasks.

A later kind of bottle that is being collected today is the

Historical Flasks

character bottle. That name is given to generally small bottles for liquor, perfume, or other use, which are shaped in the form of a human, animal, bird, fish, or any other "character" except a bottle. Some of these were made in the 1870's, many are much more recent. They are more frequently found in colored and opaque glass than in clear. In contrast with the historical flasks which are distinctively American, character bottles are often of European make.

Cup Plates

Cup plates are small plates about 2½ to 4 inches in diameter with a depressed center wide enough to accommodate the base of a cup. From about 1815 or 1820 to the early 1850's, it was the custom to set one's cup on a cup plate while one drank from the deep saucer.

Cup plates were made first in china, and in the 1820's a few were made in blown glass. When glass pressing was invented about 1825, cup plates were one of the first products made by the new process. They were put out in quantity by both eastern and midwestern glasshouses, as well as some European, for a quarter-century.

Today they are a favorite with many collectors. Being small, they have the appeal of all miniatures; they are easy to keep; they are often brilliant and jewel-like in their small-scale designs; and they are almost infinite in their variety. Many designs are conventional, such as sunbursts, hearts, and arabesques. Many have some historical or patriotic connotations—eagles, ships, or portrait busts of important personages. Some 800 designs are listed.

Milk or Milk-White Glass

Milk or milk-white glass is the common name for opaque-white glass. Of ancient origin, it was revived in the 1700's by English glassmakers in their effort to compete with porcelain, which was a fashionable novelty. At Bristol, milk glass, blown in handsome vases, was sometimes decorated like porcelain, with fine enamel painting. It was also made at other English glasshouses and throughout Europe in both the 1700's and 1800's.

Much more familiar than blown milk glass are the pressed wares made in opaque white in the 1870's, 1880's, and later. They include plates, bowls, and all the other table forms, vases and ornamental wares, bottles, lamps and candlesticks. In addition there is a variety of novelties, such as covered dishes in animal shapes, hats, shoes, and slippers. Many of the plates, bowls, vases, and compotes have lacy or "openwork" edges.

Milk glass varies greatly in quality of metal, in degree of whiteness, and in opacity. Akin to it are the opalescent tones, and the old name for it is *opal* ware. Some people nowadays use the term milk glass as a synonym not for white but for opaque, and speak of green milk glass or black milk glass. This usage seems unnecessarily confusing and inaccurate; opaque is a perfectly good word.

Opaque-white glass in combination with an opaque color produced what is called *mosaic, marble,* or more commonly *slag glass.* The color and white are mixed together but incompletely blended so that they form swirls and shaded stripings very like strongly figured marble. The color most commonly found this way in combination with opaque white is purple, but blue, green, orange, and brown also occur. Pieces were usually pressed, though occasionally blown, and include novelty forms as well as tablewares and vases.

Paperweights

The colorful and often extremely intricate glass paperweights have a special place in the hearts of many collectors. Examples appeared in Venice before 1840, reviving an old Venetian filigree technique. Soon they were produced in France, where Baccarat, St. Louis, and Clichy put out fine specimens in the 1840's and early 1850's. These are often initialed and dated obscurely within the tiny elements of the design.

In England they were made chiefly at Bristol, Stourbridge, Nailsea, and London. The best examples date from the 1840's to the 1870's. The glassmaking centers in Bohemia, Germany, and Belgium also contributed their share of paperweights during that period.

In this country they were made after the mid-century

at various glassworks in New England, New York, New Jersey, and the Pittsburgh region, especially after the Civil War and on into the 1900's. The nineteenth-century types are still made today and too often sold, with or without intent to deceive, as "early."

The *millefiori* or thousand-flowers type has, as its name implies, a cluster of tiny flower-like forms within its clear-glass shell. These were composed of small cross-sections of long canes of varicolored glass. This technique was also used in making such other ornamental objects as bottles, vases, and door-knobs.

The *flower* and *fruit* type of paperweight has a larger, fully modeled flower or piece of fruit, or a cluster of these forms, encased within the clear glass or embedded on top of it. Similar in type are the rare examples with snakes or lizards as motifs.

The *latticinio* type is sometimes combined with one of these other types, sometimes used alone. It consists of a latticework or network of fine white or colored threads within the clear ball.

The *sulphide* or *crystallo-ceramic* type has a cameo-like medallion, usually a bust portrait, encased within it. Though made actually of white china clay, these bas-reliefs have a silvery appearance as seen through the clear or colored glass surrounding them. They were produced by a technique called *cameo incrustation* developed in Bohemia in the mid-1700's and perfected in the early and mid-1800's. The name of the English glass manufacturer Apsley Pellatt is particularly associated with the process because he patented it in England in 1819, but it was also used in France, Germany, and Bohemia, and somewhat in America after 1825. Sulphides appear in tumbler bases, jewelry, vases, and other forms as well as paperweights.

In more elaborate paperweights the smooth surface of the ball was cut in facets. *Overlay* paperweights were also made, and the rare double-overlay examples are particularly desirable.

Pattern Glass

Pattern glass is the name given to the pressed glass tablewares produced in matching sets after 1840, and in greatest quantity in the 1870's and 1880's. They were all made by mechanical pressing and should not be confused with pattern-molded wares or with the patterns of blown-three-mold glass, all of which are more fully described in the first part of this chapter.

Neither is the name pattern glass applied to the earlier lacy glass ware with finely stippled backgrounds, even though, like pattern glass, lacy glass was produced by mechanical pressing, has recognizable patterns, and was made in numerous matching forms for table use.

Pattern glass was an inexpensive substitute for cut glass and many patterns are rather like cut-glass designs. The earlier ones were often made in good-quality flint glass, mostly uncolored. After the Civil War when the cheaper lime glass was adopted, patterns became fussier, coarser, more colorful, and more numerous. Pattern glass itself became cheaper. You may hear people refer to the late patterns derogatively as "baking-powder glass" because it was sometimes, but certainly not always, given away as premiums with baking powder or some other household product.

Pattern glass varies a great deal in the quality of both patterns and metal. It was made by many American glasshouses, of which the leading ones were Bakewell and Company, McKee and Brothers, Bryce Brothers, George Duncan and Sons, Adams and Company, United States Glass Company, all in Pittsburgh; Hobbs, Brockunier and Company in Wheeling, West Virginia; Boston and

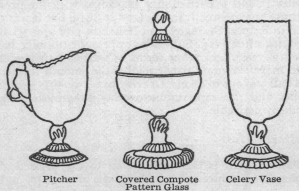

Pitcher Covered Compote Celery Vase
Pattern Glass

Sandwich Glass Company and New England Glass Company in Massachusetts; Challinor, Taylor and Company, Tarentum, Pennsylvania; and James Gillinder and Sons in Philadelphia and Greensburg, Pennsylvania. Some of the same patterns were made by different firms, with little or no variation.

Pattern glass was made in all the forms for table use which had previously been made in other materials—drinking vessels in many sizes, covered and uncovered bowls and compotes, plates and platters, salts and sugar bowls, creamers and other pitchers. In addition it was made in new shapes to fill many purposes, such as celery vases, spoonholders, dishes for butter, honey, mustard, pickles, sauce, or almost anything else. Not all these forms were made in every pattern, however.

It would be impossible to begin to list here the hundreds of patterns that have been identified. They have been thoroughly catalogued by Ruth Webb Lee and may be found illustrated and discussed in her books. In some cases the names by which patterns are known are the trade names originally used by the manufacturers, but many have acquired new designations now generally used by collectors. Some years ago Mrs. Lee listed in *The Magazine* ANTIQUES as "the popular ten" in pattern glass: *bellflower, blackberry, daisy and button, horn of plenty, lion, rose in snow, thousand eye, three face, westward-ho,* and *wildflower.*

Stemmed Glasses

In wineglasses and other stemmed glasses one can find virtually every technique for making and decorating glass exemplified, and in their shapes they present a chronological sequence of form. Many of the early European stemmed glasses are particularly interesting for their engraved or enameled decoration which frequently had patriotic or historic connotations. The so-called Jacobite glasses, for instance, made chiefly between 1740 and 1750, were for the secret use of political societies in England and Scotland, formed in loyalty to the "Old Pretender" James and his sons who tried to regain the British throne for the house of Stuart.

Disregarding such added decoration, however, we can classify stemmed glasses in certain groups according to the shapes of bowls, stems, and feet. There are many minor variations but the main types are illustrated here, with the approximate dates when they first appeared. Actually the dates overlap for a good many years, for one style did not disappear immediately when a new one came in.

Wineglasses are the most numerous of the stemmed forms. There are also, of course, stemmed glasses for ale, champagne, cordials, water, and other beverages; sweet-meat dishes; and some bowls and vases. Candlestick forms are also related to these stem forms.

In English eighteenth-century wineglasses the earliest *stems* are *baluster,* that is, shaped with a knob or knop below the bowl or above the foot. The shaping of the baluster varies greatly. Stems with some such shaping continued until about 1770. Plain *straight* stems were made from 1740 to the same date. In some, called airtwist, cotton-twist, and so on, threads of air or of white or colored glass form delicate spirals. After 1760 stems were more likely to be faceted by cutting.

Stems were sometimes blown or molded separately and applied, sometimes were pulled out from the same gather of glass as the bowl, in which case they are called *drawn stems.*

The commonest forms of *bowl* are conical, flaring, or deep and rounded at the base. Others are bell-shape, waisted or tapering in the center, or nearly globular. The

1710   1720   1730   1740   1750
Stemmed Glasses

straight-sided and flat-bottomed type called bucket-shape is seen in eighteenth-century glasses with a long stem, but with a shorter, knopped stem is characteristic of the 1820's to 1840's.

Feet were customarily fashioned separately and applied. A *domed* foot is raised in the center. A *folded* foot has the edge turned under. Feet, like stems and bowls, were often faceted after about 1760.

Early American blown wineglasses are simpler than English. Twist stems were apparently not made here, and glasses with elaborate engraving and cutting are few. There are a good many plain little glasses, however, with conical or bucket bowl, drawn or knopped stem, flat or folded foot, and perhaps with sparse floral engraving or fan cutting. These must have been made here in some quantity from the early 1800's on.

When pattern glass came in, stemmed glasses came with it, in many sizes, forms, and patterns. The shapes are not, however, as varied as the patterns. Wineglasses and goblets usually had oval bowls, and stems were relatively short. Through the same period blown glasses continued to be made. Those of the second half of the 1800's were often very delicate, with exaggeratedly long, thin stems, and decorated with engraving, enameling, and gilding. Many of these came from France and Bohemia.

Types of Art Glass

The name *art glass* covers a great variety of ornamental wares developed in the last two decades of the 1800's, usually in elaborate shapes. Some simulated other ma-

1760   1780   1820   1840   1860

Stemmed Glasses

terials like china, stone, or shell; some imitated ancient types of glass. They were chiefly freeblown, sometimes pattern-molded, and occasionally pressed. The two major types are shaded and iridescent.

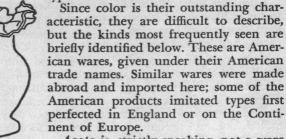

Since color is their outstanding characteristic, they are difficult to describe, but the kinds most frequently seen are briefly identified below. These are American wares, given under their American trade names. Similar wares were made abroad and imported here; some of the American products imitated types first perfected in England or on the Continent of Europe.

Art Glass Vase

Agata is, strictly speaking, not a ware but a finish applicable to any glass though used principally for *amberina* and *peach blow*. It gave a mottled surface with slight iridescence. Examples are not common.

Amberina, a transparent glass, shading, bottom to top, from yellow-amber to ruby; usually pattern-molded. It was made in the 1880's by the New England Glass Company and midwestern glass factories. A similar glass made by the Mount Washington Glass Company was called *rose amber.*

Aurene, an iridescent ware rather similar to favrile; made by Frederick Carder of the Steuben Glass Works in the early 1900's.

Burmese, an opaque shaded glass found with both dull and shiny finish, shading from yellow or orange to pink or rose at the top. Made by the Mount Washington Glass Company of New Bedford.

Cameo Glass is not strictly an art glass, since it revived an ancient Roman technique instead of being a late nineteenth-century invention, but it was contemporary with the art wares and appealed to similar tastes. It is a kind of cased glass in which the outer layer, opaque and unusually thick, is not faceted but rather sculptured —cut away in such a manner as to leave cameo-like designs in relief. The technique was adopted in England in the 1870's where it was used into the 1900's for vases, bowls, and such ornamental pieces, in classical or floral

designs. Leading makers were John Northwood and
George Woodall, associated with Thomas Webb & Sons
of Stourbridge. A type of cameo glass with naturalistic
motifs was also made by Emile Gallé of Nancy, in France.

Favrile is the trade name given by Louis C. Tiffany
to his richly-colored blown wares whose iridescence sug-
gests that of ancient glass that has been buried in the
earth. Besides ornamental pieces, like bowls and vases
and lampshades, it was made in plates, dessert dishes,
drinking vessels, and some other table forms. Pieces are
marked on the base with the initials *LCT* and sometimes also the name *Favrile*.

Kew Blas, originated by the Union Glass Works of
Somerville, Massachusetts, is a type of iridescent satin
glass similar to favrile. The name is an anagram of *W. S.
Blake,* the name of the works' manager in the late 1800's
and early 1900's when the type was being made.

Lutz Glass, see *Striped Glass.*

Mary Gregory Glass, see *Painted Glass.*

Mercury Glass, see *Silvered Glass.*

Mother-of-Pearl Glass, see *Satin Glass.*

Painted Glass. Painting or enameling and gilding frequently gave added embellishment to art glass, as they
had done to earlier types. In this case naturalistic motifs,
rosettes, and garlands are the most common designs, but
some quite elaborate landscape and ship designs were
also done, in many colors. A type with pictures of children
is often called *Mary Gregory glass,* after a woman reputed
to have specialized in such decoration at the Sandwich
factory.

Peach Blow, an imitation of
the fine Chinese porcelain
called *peachbloom,* is an
opaque glass shaded in a variety of tones, from white or
cream to rose, from red to yellow, from blue to pink; with
either dull or shiny finish.
Peach blow was made by the
Mount Washington Glass Company, and also at Pittsburgh
and Wheeling. A similar glass

Tiffany Glass Dish

made by the New England Glass Company was called *wild rose*.

Pomona, a transparent glass of which part of the surface is stippled by etching, and stained with yellow.

Quezal, an iridescent opaque glass made about 1917 at Brooklyn, New York, in imitation of Tiffany's favrile; sometimes pattern-molded, and always marked *Quezal*.

Rose Amber, see *Amberina*.

Satin or *Mother-of-Pearl Glass* is the name given to various wares made after 1885 which have a satiny, mat finish achieved by an acid vapor. They occur in many colors, often combinations of shaded colors. Usually they are cased glass, opaque within transparent, or vice versa. The core is molded in swirls, diamonds, or other patterns.

Silvered or *Mercury Glass* antedates the types more properly classed as art wares, having been perfected in Europe in the 1840's and produced in America by 1853. It is clear glass blown double with a space between the layers which is filled with a silver solution. Table and ornamental wares, knobs for doors, curtains and furniture, bell pulls, lamp bases and reflectors, and paperweights were made in silvered glass, which was sometimes etched, engraved, or painted. Some forms continued to be made up to 1900 but its real vogue was over by the 1880's when art wares came on the market.

Spangled Glass is a cased glass characterized by spangles or flakes of mica in the inner layer which reflect and sparkle through the colored outer layer. Made in Wheeling, West Virginia, and Connecticut.

Striped Glass, a thin transparent glass striped with colored twists in the Venetian style. Often called *Lutz glass* today, this type of glass was indeed made at Sandwich by Nicholas Lutz, a French glassblower who worked there from 1869 to 1888. However, he did not make all of it. The type was also made earlier in Europe, and perhaps by other American factories at the same time, and has been made up to the present day.

Vasa Murrhina is a kind of "metallized" glass which appears flecked with gold or silver; the effect is given by flakes of mica coated with metal which are suspended within the transparent colored glass. Made at Sandwich.

Wild Rose, see *Peach Blow*.

Caleb Hopkins, Nath.ˡ Barber, John White

No. 45.
Wilkes & Liberty

5. Silver

In 1768 Paul Revere of Boston made a silver bowl to memorialize the daring defiance of royal authority by 92 members of the Massachusetts House of Representatives. The bowl was simple and elegant in form, and around its smooth surface was engraved, among symbols of Liberty, "To the Memory of the Glorious Ninety-Two" who "Voted not to Rescind" a protest to King George III against recent measures restricting trade.

This vote, which preceded "the shot heard 'round the world" by seven years, was one of the overt acts that led to the American War for Independence. The bowl that commemorates it, known as the Sons of Liberty bowl, is still in existence, proudly preserved by the Museum of Fine Arts in Boston. It has been called the most historic piece of American silver.

History has often been written in silver. Because the lustrous metal has always seemed particularly appropriate for presentation or commemorative pieces, many handsome forms are inscribed for special occasions. Some commemorate significant events. Some carry the names of past owners, famous names that add their own luster to the pieces. Personal history, too, is told in silver. The initials and dates on a piece given for a baptism or a marriage often help fill in gaps in a family tree.

Like china, silver did not come into general use as tableware until well along in the 1700's. It was costly, so

Bowl by Paul Revere, 1768

that even then it was not for common use. The modern idea that every bride is entitled to a silver service did not develop until the nineteenth century had introduced new manufacturing methods and quantity production. Before that there was no possibility of simply selecting the style or pattern you liked from a large stock of ready-made pieces.

It was the nineteenth century too that introduced inexpensive plated silver. Sheffield plate had been made since the 1740's, but the invention of electroplating about 1840 put it off the market and brought plated silver within the reach of average people.

Before that, silver had always been a luxury. It was a rich metal, and expert craftsmanship was lavished on bringing out its full beauty. Simple forms were emphasized by smooth surfaces and accented by raised decoration that caught the light. The handsome covered cups, bowls and plates, tankards and other drinking vessels, into which silver was worked were often elaborately ornamented and even covered with gilt.

While these were used by the few who could afford to own them, they were not primarily utilitarian, nor were they merely decorative. They were symbols of wealth; they also were wealth itself in a tangible form. For in the days when there were no savings banks, people took their silver coins to the silversmith and had him convert them into usable and decorative objects. Thus owning silver was an investment, and the early smiths were in a sense bankers.

The silversmiths in colonial America were often prominent members of the community. John Hull, one of the first, was made master of the mint of the Massachusetts Bay Colony when that was established in 1652. He it was who coined the pine-tree shillings that have become a part of New England tradition. He and his partner, Robert Sanderson, also made church silver, porringers, spoons, tankards, and cups.

Boston was the first of the colonial towns to become prosperous enough to support a group of silversmiths. John Coney, Jeremiah Dummer, Edward Winslow, and William Rouse were others working

Pine-Tree Shilling

there before 1700 and producing some of the fine early silver that is in our museums today.

Before the Revolution there were many more. Their names include John and Benjamin Burt, Jacob and Nathaniel Hurd, Daniel Henchman, William Cowell, but the most famous of them all is Paul Revere. He would probably not be so universally known if Longfellow had not romanticized his midnight ride, but he was a worthy craftsman and a versatile one. Besides making excellent silver, he engraved pictures, cast bells, and manufactured copper. As a substantial citizen he had his portrait painted by John Singleton Copley, the best artist in Boston at the time.

New York also became a silvermaking center in the 1600's. There we find many Dutch and French names among the leading smiths. Before 1750 there were Gerrit Onckelbag, Bartholomew LeRoux, Jacobus van der Spiegel, Benjamin Wynkoop, Peter van Dyck, Adrian Bancker, Henricus and Jacob Boelen, Simeon Soumain, and numerous others.

Philadelphia, established later than Boston and New York, was later in achieving prosperity. By the mid-1700's, however, its Quaker merchants were building handsome houses and equipping them with the most luxurious furnishings in the Colonies. Philip Syng, Jr., Joseph Richardson, Sr. and Jr., Abraham Dubois, Joseph Lownes, were among those making fine silver for Philadelphia homes in the latter 1700's.

The total list of silversmiths working in colonial America is many hundreds long, and they were scattered in various smaller towns as well as the major cities. There were relatively few in the South, where fine household goods were often brought from England or the North.

These craftsmen were trained by a long apprenticeship, and many of them were highly skilled. Some of the pieces they made are as elegant and finely wrought as what was being done in Europe at the time, though much of it is simpler. In general, American smiths followed English traditions, except in New York where Dutch influence was strong and local characteristics were developed.

The objects they made most frequently up to about 1750 were drinking vessels—beakers, tankards, mugs, and handled cups. After about 1725 the various forms used in the serving of tea were developed. Pieces for the dining table became more numerous and varied as luxuries for the table became more plentiful and called for suitable vessels in which to serve them. By the early 1800's domestic silver was made in forms to meet most of the uses it serves today, though new ones and variations on the old continued to appear throughout the nineteenth century.

The old pieces reflect the taste of their times, and follow the general trend of changing styles that we can see in furniture and all the other decorative arts. Thus we can recognize the "periods" of silver too, by means of shapes and types of decoration.

An acquaintance with the historic styles is not necessary in order to enjoy old silver, for the metal itself and the artistry it shows are appealing and satisfying. Understanding their background, however, increases your appreciation of both old silver and new. Many of the early styles are constantly reproduced in modern silver, for they are perennially pleasing.

Broadly speaking, silver styles passed from relative simplicity in the early 1700's, to an ornamental rococo in the mid-century, then to an adaptation of the classic in the late 1700's and early 1800's which was expressed in terms of elegance and grace. After 1820 silver gradually grew heavier and more massive, with classic or naturalistic motifs in form and ornament. Before the mid-century it had again become rococo: shapes were more curved, more complicated, and there was even greater emphasis on naturalistic decoration. By the last third of the 1800's there was a new classic trend, with inspiration borrowed from the Italian Renaissance. This development over two centuries paralleled that in furniture, and similarities between the two are not hard to see, particularly in decorative details.

Silver made before 1700, of whatever nationality, is scarce. Of what was made after 1700, English silver is more plentiful here than that of any other country. It has been used in America from earliest times and is, of course, still being imported—both antique and modern. That of the Georgian period *(1714-1830)* offers all sorts of attractive and usable forms, for in this period silver passed from occasional display in only the wealthiest homes to general use among the well-to-do.

Among Georgian silversmiths the name of Paul Lamerie stands out. He was an exceptional craftsman who worked in London over a long period, from 1717 to 1751. Paul Storr was a leading London maker from 1792 until after 1830. A great favorite among collectors is Hester Bateman, the best-known woman silversmith. Between 1774 and 1789 she worked in London producing silver with the elegant line and refined decoration of the neo-classic style. Other Batemans, Peter and Ann, William, and Jonathan, carried on the craft until 1840.

American silver is more costly than English pieces of comparable style and age. This is because there is less of it, and because American antiques of all kinds are at a premium among American collectors.

Any silver made after about 1825, when new methods of production began to replace the old craftsmanship, is priced on a considerably lower scale than the earlier. In fact, it has not been considered "collectible" until recently. It will doubtless be more appreciated as it grows older.

Old silver has the individuality that all handmade things have. It also has a soft richness of color quite different from that of modern silver. This is not just a romantic illusion on the part of people who like antiques. The repeated heating which was necessary in making old silver created a bloom on the surface which is called the *skin* or *fireskin*. To preserve this warm color, old silver should be polished with great care and never buffed. The modern process of buffing gives a high gloss but it removes the skin and leaves the surface as cold and white as new silver.

Silvermaking Techniques

Up to the late 1700's all silver bowls, pitchers, drinking vessels, and the other forms known as hollow ware were made by the method called *raising*. Starting with a flat sheet of silver which he had cast from molten coin and other odd bits of silver available, the smith literally raised the piece into shape by hammering it against iron forms called stakes. During this process the piece had to be repeatedly heated, or annealed, to keep it from cracking. After it had been given its final form it was polished to remove the hammer marks but often they are still faintly visible on old silver.

About 1825 the old technique of raising silver began to be replaced by new methods which led to greatly increased production. *Spinning* on a lathe was the most important of the mechanical aids which presently all but eliminated the old hand processes.

Casting produced certain essential elements like feet, handles, and hinges, and also certain decorative devices that were applied with solder. There were various other techniques used in the decoration of early silver:

Repoussé

Repoussé, which means literally pushed back, is done by hammering from within and produces a design in relief on the outer surface of the piece which is also visible in reverse on the inside. The English name for it, less often used, is *embossing*. the outer surface. It too is done with hammers and

Chasing gives a somewhat similar effect, though the design is usually in lower relief or is depressed below chisels, but working from the outside rather than the inside of the piece. In both repoussé and chasing it is always the whole thickness of the silver that has been displaced to form the design.

Gadrooning, done by the repoussé technique, is a reeding, vertical or slanted or even spiraled. It was a popular decoration for the base or body of a piece in the late 1600's and early 1700's. Gadrooned borders were much used in the late 1700's and in the 1800's. These were often cast and applied instead of being hammered out.

Fluting is the opposite of gadrooning, the grooves being depressed instead of raised.

Engraving produced the inscription on the Sons of Liberty bowl, which is shown at the head of this chapter.

Engraving

With engraving, in contrast to repoussé and chasing, part of the silver surface is actually scraped away with sharp tools or burins to form the design. While the outer surface shows the design clearly, the inside remains smooth. Coats of arms, initials, and inscriptions were always engraved. These, incidentally, were not merely for show but were identification of ownership in case of theft.

Bright-cut engraving, a type popular in the late 1700's and early 1800's, made a design not with smooth, even lines but with short, sharp chips and gouges which gave bright contrast to the smooth surface.

Piercing is just what the name implies: designs are formed by holes cut clear through the silver in decorative shapes. Piercing was used principally on porringer handles, strainers, and on the raised edges or galleries of trays.

Cut-card work is an attractive but less frequent type of decoration. It occurs in English and in French silver of the first half of the 1700's, and more rarely in American up to the time of the Revolution. It consists of a thin layer of silver cut in an ornamental pattern and superimposed on the surface of a piece, usually around a finial or the base of a handle or spout.

Cut-card work around the finial, gadrooning around the edge of the cover, and piercing in the handles are all illustrated in the porringer pictured at the right.

Porringer with Gadrooning, Piercing, and Cut-Card

Major Forms in Early American Silver

Up to the mid-1700's the major forms in American silver were drinking vessels.

Beakers are handleless cups. The typical early form is tall, slender, and tapering, with a flaring lip and a molded base. By the late 1700's it had become more squat and straight-sided. This shape, often with a molding around base and top, persisted up to the mid-1800's in the South, where examples were given as trophies at agricultural fairs. They are now often called julep cups.

Beakers
early 1700's, late 1700's

The *tankard* is a cylindrical vessel with handle and hinged cover, and a little thumbpiece for raising the cover. Seventeenth-century examples appear fairly mammoth today. In the early 1700's they were somewhat smaller but still often had full quart capacity. The body at this time was chunky, the top flat, the stout curved handle had a little kickout at the bottom, and there was usually engraved or applied decoration on cover and handle and around the base.

By the mid-1700's the body was more elongated and often circled by a narrow molding called a midrib; the top might be domed and capped by a finial. Decoration was largely confined to moldings. By 1800 tankards in silver had gone out of date.

Tankard, early 1700's

Tankard, mid-1700's

Mugs, or *cans* to use the old name, are really tankards without covers, and in general follow tankard design. A form that appeared before the mid-1700's is more usual in mugs than in tankards: the curved, modified pear shape on a molded foot, with hollow or flat handle in scroll form.

Two-handled cups were made for both use and display. The *caudle cup* was a typical form shortly before and after 1700 and was for drinking caudle, a hot spiced wine beverage. Examples are much rarer in American than in English silver and represent the work of some of our finest early smiths. Later in the 1700's two-handled cups were larger and taller, handsome footed pieces with heavy scrolled handles and often a domed cover.

One of the commonest forms in silver is the *porringer.* In America it was used for a great variety of purposes throughout the 1600's and 1700's. Its chief variation is in the form and ornamentation of the handle, which was cast, pierced, and applied. Early handles had geometrical designs; after 1725 they were commonly pierced in scrolls forming what we call the *keyhole* design. Two-handled and even four-handled porringers were made in Continental and English silver, with covers, but the American type had only one handle and rarely a cover.

By the mid-1700's, the drinking of tea and coffee had attained the importance of a social cult. These exotic beverages were first introduced into England from the Orient in the early 1600's, but they did not become generally available and popular for nearly a century. Once adopted, the new custom required new equipment, and had its effect on silver forms as it did on furniture and ceramics.

Caudle Cup, 1700

Two-Handled Cup, 1740

Teapots show the sequence of style changes as clearly as any other form. The earliest ones in silver, like those in china, were small, for tea was scarce and precious. Little spherical pots were made in the first half of the 1700's, sometimes mounted on a low foot, with straight or curved spouts, and scrolled handles usually of wood.

Another early teapot form was the pear shape with high domed top, which had a rather squat lower section and usually a molded rib encircling the body where it narrowed. Both spout and handle were curved. By gradual evolution the pear shape became inverted, with the bulge above the slender curved section below, mounted on a higher foot, and repeating its graceful curves in spout, handle, and shape of lid.

Toward the end of the 1700's straight-sided oval pots on a flat base appeared. This form was often given variety by fluting the sides. The pot frequently stood on a small oval footed tray.

With the early 1800's this rather severe cylindrical teapot acquired new curves in the so-called boat shape, often decorated with horizontal bands stamped in a pattern and applied.

Later the body of the pot was decorated with gadrooning or fluting. By the mid-1800's it had become ornate with naturalistic motifs in relief.

Tea kettles are not common in American silver. Produced chiefly in the mid-1700's, examples are related to the spherical teapots or the inverted pear shape, with the addition of a bail, or drop handle, and a standard with lamp.

Toward 1800 the *tea urn* appeared, replacing the kettle. It embodies the pure classic form, with slender curves, high cover topped by a finial, and two graceful handles.

Sugar was scarce in early days, so early *sugar bowls* are small. Examples in silver appear along with tea drinking, and the forms show a relation to those of teapots. Earlier there had been a few *sugar boxes*, oval, ornately decorated, with hinged covers that had a lock. In the sugar bowls of the 1700's we can trace, as in teapots, the progression from the spherical form—modified to fill the specific function—through the pear shape and inverted pear shape, to the classic urn shape.

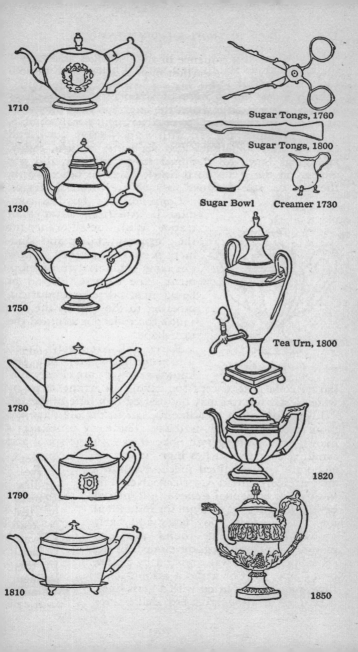

1710

Sugar Tongs, 1760

Sugar Tongs, 1800

Sugar Bowl   Creamer 1730

1730

1750

Tea Urn, 1800

1780

1790

1820

1810

1850

Creamers follow a similar development. The pear shape sometimes stands on a molded base, sometimes on three little scroll legs.

Early *sugar tongs* were of scissors type—two pieces hinged at the middle. From the late 1700's on, they were made of a single thin piece of silver, bent nearly double.

The matching *tea set,* with teapot, sugar bowl, and creamer, and sometimes also tea kettle or urn, caddy, and dregs bowl, all designed to go together, did not appear on the scene until nearly 1800. In other words, the first tea sets designed as such are in classic forms.

Coffeepot, 1800

Coffeepots are far less common in American silver than teapots. With due allowance for their generally taller and slimmer proportions, they follow the same general style development. The earliest, instead of being spherical, were cylindrical, tapering to the top. In the late 1700's the coffeepot assumed the urn shape.

Rarer still are early American *chocolate pots*. The few known examples are closely similar to coffeepots, except for having an arrangement by which a stirring rod may be inserted in a hole in the lid.

Like many other condiments, salt in the old days was more precious than it is today. The early container is known as a *standing salt*. Shaped like a large spool and standing over five inches high, it was an elaborate and dignified piece. Examples are extremely rare in American silver. The low oval or octagonal *trencher salt*, placed beside the trencher or plate for individual use, was used in the 1600's and early 1700's. By 1730 the round salt cup mounted on curved legs developed. In the classic period this was replaced by a slim, oval shape, with or without a foot, sometimes pierced and fitted with a glass liner.

Caster, 1740

Casters or *dredgers* were shakers for

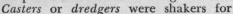

pepper, spice, or sugar. They range in height from about three inches to nine. From the simple cylindrical form, with or without handle, of the late 1600's and early 1700's, developed the straight-sided octagonal form which appeared in the early 1700's and persisted for years. The pear shape on a foot was also adapted to casters and given a high domed cover which was pierced for sifting, often in a very decorative design. Casters were often in sets of three, two small and one large.

Detail of Scroll-Edge Tray, 1750

A favorite type of *tray, salver,* or *waiter* is that of the mid-1700's which has a heavy scrolled or "piecrust" edge, like some Chippendale tables of the same time. Often it has shells at the notches, and usually three or four small scrolled feet. Round salvers of the 1730's to 1780's, and square or rectangular ones with rounded corners, had a gadrooned edge or other decorative border, and engraved or chased decoration within it. The classic type of the late 1700's and early 1800's often had a beaded edge or pierced gallery, and handles.

Punchbowls, sauceboats, tea caddies and *strainers, pitchers, snuffboxes,* are only a few of the other objects made by silversmiths in America. The *monteith* was a punchbowl with notched edge, named, they say, for a Scotsman

Monteith Bowl, 1760

who wore a cloak with a scalloped edge. The purpose of the notches on the bowl was to suspend footed glasses so as to chill them.

A major item in early silver was *candlesticks,* and related to them are *tapersticks, candelabra,* and *snuffers.* Silver used in churches, some of which was originally made for domestic use, includes beakers, large plates called *patens,* and *flagons* which are like tankards only taller and thinner and with a spout. Many old churches still preserve their early silver.

Knives, Forks, and Spoons

The form of spoons has undergone great changes since the first silversmiths began to work in America. At that time the usual form had a much wider bowl than we are now accustomed to, almost round, in fact, and the handle was stiffly straight and short. The development through the 1700's and early 1800's was toward a form increasingly comfortable to handle and use, and toward lighter weight. The bowl became more oval, or egg-shaped. The handle became wider, thinner, and longer.

Spoons of the late 1600's and early 1700's had handles with a trifid (three-pointed) or a wavy end. Presently developed the round-tipped handle, upcurved at the end, with a ridge down the center, which was the typical form until after the mid-century. To strengthen the junction between the bowl and handle there was usually a long "rat-tail" from the handle down the back of the bowl.

By the 1730's or so this reinforcement became abbreviated and took the form of a single or double drop. About this time teaspoons appeared, smaller than earlier spoons, to go with the small teacups of the time.

After about 1760 the handle end began to turn down instead of up, and bowls became narrower and more pointed. By the 1790's spoons were thin and light.

Up to that time, the decoration of spoons was often

Spoons, back and front

1650   1690   1700   1750   1760

on the backs of the bowls. Initials or crests signifying ownership were engraved on the backs of the handles.

In the 1790's and early 1800's bright-cut engraving frequently decorated the front of spoon handles, which were slender and tapering, pointed or rounded at the end, or clipped off in a "coffin end." By this time spoons were made in a complete range of sizes, from tiny mustard and salt spoons to large serving spoons.

With the early 1800's the bowl continued thin and pointed, while the handle widened into the form descriptively called *fiddle shape,* which was very generally made through the 1840's and even later. Many families have some heirloom pieces of this kind, thin and light in weight, engraved with script initials, and stamped on the back with the name of the maker or seller.

Popular decorations on the fiddle shape from about 1810 to 1830 were the *sheaf of wheat* and *basket of flowers,* stamped or cast in relief near the end of the handle. The *thread* design which has a ridge or thread outlining the fiddle shape was first made about this time and is still a favorite today. It sometimes has a shell decorating the end of the handle.

After about 1830 the raised designs on handles of spoons and other flatware became much more varied, since they were usually stamped or cast instead of being engraved or chased as in the past. The spoon shape remained fairly standard, an oval bowl and a tapering

Spoons, back and front

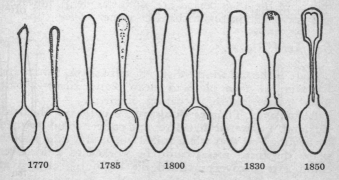

1770   1785   1800   1830   1850

handle with rounded, upturned end, and innovations were chiefly in the designs that more or less covered the handle. After 1860 there was a taste for heavy pieces ornately decorated in high relief.

Forks were scarcely known before about 1660 and did not come into common use until nearly a century later. Examples made in America before the end of the 1700's are rare. They usually have only two or three tines, and their handles correspond to those of contemporary spoons. Four-tined forks were not customary much before 1800, though they did exist earlier.

Early American knives are as rare as forks. In English silver the pistol handle, hollow and shaped like a pistol grip, became popular for knives and to some extent for forks in the mid-1700's, and continued in use until late in the century. The knives have steel blades, very long and curved at the end.

Steel knives and forks with bone handles were in common use throughout the 1800's. Handles of ivory or porcelain were fashionable before 1800 and continued in the following century.

Knife and Fork, 1760

Such specialized flatware forms as oyster forks, salad forks, butter knives, fish knives and forks, iced tea spoons, were developments of the 1800's, chiefly after 1850. The souvenir "demi-tasse" spoons in novelty shapes, often enameled and gilded, were a fashion of the 1890's. Some of the bright-cut teaspoons of the 1800 period are almost as small, however, and serve admirably with after-dinner coffee cups.

Sheffield Plate

Plate is the old word for silver—solid silver. Nowadays, however, we take plate to mean plated silver—a base metal covered with a coating of silver.

About 1742 Thomas Boulsover, a cutler of Sheffield, England, discovered that silver and copper could be fused by heating and that when rolled out into a thin smooth plate, the fused metal could be worked as solid silver could. His discovery marked the beginning of a great industry, which thrived for just a century until it was superseded by the cheaper method of electroplating.

The earliest objects made in Sheffield plate were buttons, and then small boxes for snuff and tobacco. Eventually most of the articles for use and decoration made in silver at the time were also produced in Sheffield plate —candlesticks and candelabra in abundance, teapots, coffeepots, and presently full tea and coffee services, trays, cake and fruit baskets, inkstands, tureens and covered dishes, wine coolers, salts and coasters, and other forms too many to enumerate. Shapes and decorative treatments followed those of silver.

Articles composed almost entirely of thin wire, soldered together in a fragile network with only a solid base or rim, are rare in old silver, but wirework was a characteristic device in old Sheffield plate, despite the difficulties of plating copper wire with silver and working it into firm, fine shapes. Wire cake baskets and fruit baskets, made chiefly between 1790 and 1810, are specially favored items in old Sheffield.

Considering the nature of old Sheffield plate, with its very thin surface of silver, it is surprising that so much has lasted to the present in good condition. Examples are often seen, however, on which the silver is quite worn away in spots, revealing the red copper beneath. Such pieces, called "bloody," are not considered desirable, and many people have them resilvered by electroplating. While this makes them more attractive and practical, it robs them of their essential character.

Electroplate

The name Sheffield plate is often incorrectly thought to mean all silver-plated ware with a copper base, however made, but it should be reserved for the old fused and rolled plate.

Electroplate is like Sheffield plate in that it consists of a coating of silver over a base metal—but there the similarity ends. Electroplate is produced by electrolysis: in simplest terms, galvanic current set up in a bath of potassium cyanide decomposes silver and deposits it on another metal. The base metal may be copper but is usually white metal, or britannia.

Electroplating is a far cheaper process than making Sheffield plate, and lends itself to all sorts of forms and decorations which are not possible by the earlier method. That is why electroplate, introduced about 1840, soon pushed the old plate off the market, and why we find it in forms and in quantities that had never been known in silver or Sheffield.

While Sheffield plate was made almost exclusively in England, at Birmingham as well as at Sheffield, electroplate was and is made in many countries. In the United States the process was adopted soon after its discovery in England, and a great industry rapidly developed. Large quantities of both American and English electroplate of 1850-1900 are found here today, and also some Continental.

Only recently have people begun collecting electroplate. While it hardly deserves a place of honor beside a Paul Revere bowl or a Paul Lamerie coffeepot, it is practical for many purposes, and is frequently pleasing in design and workmanship. It offers the fascination of hunting for matching pieces, for, like contemporary pattern glass and Staffordshire china, electroplate was produced in matched sets that included a great variety of forms for table use.

If Sheffield plate is sometimes confused with electroplate, so is solid silver confused with both. But there are certain tests which can be applied and are sufficient in most cases:

Electroplate is heavier than Sheffield, and Sheffield is heavier than solid silver—for pieces of comparable form and size.

Sheffield usually has a softer, richer color than silver, electroplate a colder, whiter color than either. No amount of use will give electroplate the patina of solid silver.

Sheffield occurs only in styles and forms in vogue between about 1740 and 1840. The later nineteenth-century styles were made in both silver and electroplate, and reproductions of the earlier styles are made in both today.

In Sheffield it is usually possible to feel the thin rim of silver which was folded over along edges to conceal the copper base. This is not found on silver or electroplate.

Carefully joined seams where spouts and handles are applied are usually visible in Sheffield plate and in solid silver. These do not exist in electroplate where the silver covers the entire piece in an unbroken surface.

Engraving on Sheffield was done on "silver shields" let into the surface to avoid cutting through the thin plating. These can sometimes be detected by the eye; if not, they show when you blow on the piece to make a misty film. They do not occur on silver or electroplate.

Marks on Silver and Plated Wares

In England, silvermaking has been firmly regulated since the 1300's by the Worshipful Company of Goldsmiths. This guild requires every piece of silver to be assayed before it is sold, and stamped with certain *hall marks,* so called because they are put on at Goldsmiths' Hall.

These include the maker's mark, the town mark, and the date letter. At times in the past other marks have been required. For instance, between 1784 and 1890 the sovereign's head was stamped to indicate that duty had been paid. The maker's mark usually consists of his initials. The town mark for London is a leopard's head; for Edinburgh, two towers; for Dublin, a harp. The date letter is assigned according to a time-honored system by the Goldsmiths' Company. The London date letter for 1776, for example, is a small Roman a.

The explanation of all these marks is written down in various books which may be referred to by anyone who wants to decode them. Not all English maker's marks are identified, but some thousands of them are. The most complete list of them is in *English Goldsmiths and Their Marks* by Charles J. Jackson (American edition, 1950).

In America, no comparable guild regulated the silversmiths' products. Certain associations of the craftsmen appear to have existed, briefly and locally, but they exercised no such complete control as the Goldsmiths' Company. However, it was customary for American silversmiths to stamp a mark on their wares.

For a reputable craftsman, his own name was his guarantee of quality. In early days a smith's mark usually consisted of his initials, or of his surname and initial, in relief against a depressed rectangle, oval, heart, shield, or other background shape. Some such marks were used into the nineteenth century. Toward the late 1700's and more frequently in the 1800's he might add the name of the town where he worked. The best guide to these marks is *American Silversmiths and Their Marks III*, by Stephen G. C. Ensko (New York, 1948).

A silversmith might use several different marks on a single piece, marks which somewhat resemble the hall marks on English silver. These *pseudo hall marks* were used in the early 1800's. By the 1830's when silvermaking was becoming an industry rather than an independent craft, we often find silver marked with the name of the seller rather than the maker.

After 1830 the words *coin, pure coin, dollar,* or the initials *C* or *D* were sometimes stamped on silver. These do not mean that the ware was made from melted coin, as eighteenth-century silver was. They were used to indicate that the silver was of the quality of coin from the United States mint, which was .900 fine, or 900 parts pure silver out of 1000.

The word *sterling* did not come to be generally used on American silver until after 1860. It indicates that silver on which it appears is .925 fine.

Unlike English silver, Sheffield plate was not required by law to be assayed and stamped with the hall marks which guaranteed quality and revealed date, source, and maker. Some old Sheffield carries maker's marks of a different sort, but most of it does not, and a mark does not affect the value of a piece. The known marks are recorded, but approximate date is determined on the basis of technique and style.

Electroplate is not required to be marked but it frequently is. Such words as *triple* and *quadruple* indicate, of course, the thickness of the plate. Trade names and manufacturers' names are often stamped on the ware, and pseudo hall marks are occasionally used.

6. Pewter

From the days of the Pilgrims until about 1840, pewter was an almost indispensable metal in the homes of our ancestors. It was the material not only of all sorts of tablewares, but of countless useful objects like candlesticks, lamps, inkstands, picture frames, door latches, clock dials, nursing bottles, and even such odds and ends as buttons and buckles.

In Europe pewter had been made for centuries. Much of the Continental pewter—Austrian, German, Swiss, Dutch, French—is older than our own, more varied in its forms, and more highly decorative, but it is not often seen in this country. English pewter, on the whole less elaborate than the Continental, is easier to find but not so highly prized here as the rarer American.

By the time the first settlers came to America, pewter had begun to take the place of woodenware, or *treenware* as it was called, which had been the common thing for table use. To supply the new demand, trained pewterers migrated to the Colonies at an early date, bringing their molds and the other tools of their trade with them. We know from old records of a few pewterers working here before 1700, but only one piece of American pewter made before that date has been discovered. This is a spoon dated 1675, which was made near Jamestown, Virginia, and excavated there some years ago.

Pieces made between 1700 and the Revolution are scarce today, but we know that they did exist in considerable quantity. Up to the early 1800's pewter was the common tableware, and many a pine cupboard was bright with its garnish of gleaming pewter.

Pewter corrodes readily, is easily bent, and melts promptly if exposed to direct heat. That is one reason why so little of the early ware used here, both American and foreign, still exists. Another reason is that when pieces became worn they were melted down and re-worked into something new.

Pewter is an alloy composed principally of tin, with copper, antimony, bismuth, and sometimes lead, as the other ingredients. In the early days, pewtermaking con-sisted essentially of *casting* and *turning*. Molten metal was poured into a brass mold which gave a piece its form. The casting thus made was turned on a lathe, or *skimmed,* to smooth the surface. Some pieces, though not all, were then hammered, to increase their strength. Certain shapes had to be made by casting two or more parts and soldering them together.

In old pewter, incidentally, the hammer marks are often barely visible. They were left by a necessary proc-ess in the making, and were not meant for decoration. They look quite different from the intentionally large, deep hammer marks applied purely for effect in modern "arts and crafts" pewter.

About 1825 a new method of shaping pewterware was adopted, as happened at the same time in the mak-ing of silverware. It is called *spinning,* and is a way of giving shape to a thin, flat sheet of metal by pressing it, on a lathe, against a wooden form called a chuck. Spinning eliminated the casting and hammering proc-esses and made it possible to fashion lighter vessels in a greater variety of shapes. Spun pieces show no hammer marks.

About 1800 an alloy called *britannia metal,* which had been developed in England, was introduced in this country, and by 1825 had practically replaced the old pewter. It was actually a superior grade of pewter, de-veloped to meet the competition of new and relatively inexpensive kinds of china. To give the improved alloy a popular appeal, the pewterers dropped the old famil-iar name of pewter and called it britannia.

Virtually all American pewter made after about 1825 is really britannia. The metal was used for all sorts of household objects and produced in great quantities for a generation. After 1840 it was adopted as the base for electroplated silver, which gradually replaced it on American tables. From the collector's point of view, "early" American pewter means ware made before 1825.

Pewter has been called the poor man's silver, and it follows silver closely in design, though it is simpler in decoration. Engraving was done on European pewter but very rarely on American, and such techniques as chasing and repoussé were not possible on the soft pewter. While some forms common in one metal are rarely found in the other, teapots, pitchers, tankards, and other drinking vessels follow the same pattern in both pewter and silver, and both served the same purposes.

In addition to its multifarious domestic uses, pewter was also made into communion services. Church pewter includes some of the handsomest examples of the pewterer's craft —tall flagons, chalices, and patens.

By far the greatest amount of early American pewter was flatware, or *sadware,* as it used to be called—sad meaning heavy. Flatware in pewter means more than it does in silver, for it includes all the items cast in a single piece—vessels of various sizes and

Chalice, late 1700's

shapes, as well as spoons. Teapots, tankards, measures, and the other objects that had to be cast in two or more pieces and soldered together are called hollowware.

As with silver, American pewter mainly followed the successive styles of England, but most flatware necessarily clung to fairly standardized forms and does not show a marked chronological development.

American pewter plates and dishes usually have a wide, slightly curved rim with a narrow molded edge on

Flagon, late 1700's

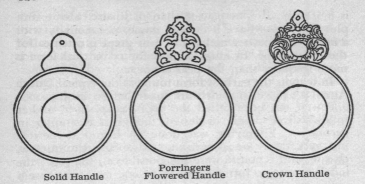

Solid Handle

Porringers
Flowered Handle

Crown Handle

the upper surface. Less common are those with a wide, smooth, flat rim, having no molding on the upper surface but a reed or molded edge on the underside. In English pewter this type is characteristic of work before the last quarter of the 1600's. In American pewter it is found in the 1700's. Basins, which have just a narrow molded rim, range in diameter from under four inches to fourteen, but the smallest and largest sizes are rare.

One of the commonest forms in pewter hollowware is the porringer. Examples differ chiefly in the shapes and ornamentation of their handles. Many pewter porringer handles have pierced geometric designs. More ornamental are those pierced in scrolled designs—what the pewterers used to call "flowered" handles. Solid handles also occur, oval or clover-shaped, with just a single hole by which the porringer could be hung on a hook. A handle common in English but rare in American porringers has a cast design—a crown or dolphin.

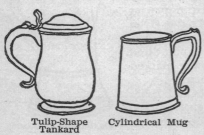

Tulip-Shape
Tankard

Cylindrical Mug

Drinking vessels, again, follow silver precedents. Beakers in the tall early form are rare in American pewter, but short, flaring ones are fairly common. The straight-sided tankard with domed top is more frequent in pewter than in silver. Later examples sometimes have a double dome, occasionally with a finial. The pewter tankard in pear shape is often called the tulip shape. In mugs or pots the cylindrical form is more frequent than the pear shape.

In teapots the earliest form found is the typical Queen Anne pear shape, which in American silver is associated with the period from about 1725 to 1750. In pewter it is rare, and marked examples are of relatively late in the century.

About 1800 pewter teapots were made in the low, tapered, cylindrical form with straight spout. By the beginning of the britannia period they had become much taller. The commonest shape had a bulging body on a high foot, and a long curved spout.

Coffeepots are extremely rare in early American pewter. Sugar bowls are rather more numerous than creamers, and both are found most often in the pear shape.

Spoons were made in great quantities. Most of those found today are of the britannia period. The molds in which spoons were cast are also seen occasionally. They are in two parts that fit together with a hole at the end for pouring in the molten metal.

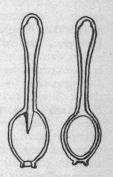

Spoon Mold

When britannia metal and the spinning process arrived in this country, the metal was fashioned in many new forms. Some, such as whale-oil lamps, were created to meet new needs. Others were attempts to introduce novelty into old utensils.

The teapot, in particular, appeared in a variety of new shapes, as well as in larger sizes. Many teapots of this period are of quart or even two-quart size, and have often been mistaken for coffeepots. Tea was much more plentiful than it had been a century before, and there was no longer any need to brew it in tiny pots. Coffeepots at this time, while more numerous than formerly, are still less common than teapots.

The large bulbous pitcher, with or without a cover,

Pewter Teapots

is a characteristic form in britannia. Others include cylindrical or straight-sided pieces, modifications of the ubiquitous pear shape, and various angular shapes that are quite different from the traditional ones in metal-wares of the 1700's. In this era of the matching tea set, we find teapots, creamers, and sugar bowls of similar design, made to be used together. Candlesticks and lamps in britannia are numerous.

Various types of maker's marks, or *touches,* are found stamped on American pewter. This was not obligatory, as it was in England where the Worshipful Company of Pewterers controlled pewter production and required marks to guarantee quality. American pewter is frequently unmarked, as is a good deal of Continental.

Marks that were used in America were sometimes the name of the pewterer, perhaps with the name of the town in which he worked; sometimes only his initials; sometimes a symbol which he adopted as his own mark of identification. A mark combining a rose and crown, for example, which is often found on English ware, was also used by colonial pewterers; after the Revolution it was replaced by various types of eagle marks.

Britannia Teapots

In early pewter marks, the letters or designs stand out in relief against a background depressed in the surface of the piece. Marks in which the letters themselves are depressed replaced the early type after about 1825.

In addition to maker's marks, American pewter sometimes carries "quality marks," such as an X, to indicate a superior grade of metal; and sometimes sets of two, three, or four small marks similar to the hall marks on English silver. Those silver hall marks, however, were required by law and indicate source and date of mak-

Britannia Pitcher, 1825

ing and quality of metal. The pseudo hall marks on American pewter merely help in identifying the maker.

The marks of American pewterers are identified, and much information about the men and their wares is also given, in Ledlie I. Laughlin's two-volume book, *Pewter in America* (Boston, 1940).

Early American pewter—that is, pre-1825—is highly valued by collectors. The work of certain makers is always prized, especially when it is clearly marked. Among these craftsmen are William Will of Philadelphia, Henry Will and Frederick Bassett of New York, Richard Lee, Sr. and Jr., of Massachusetts and Vermont, Peter Young of Albany, David Melvil of Newport, Johann Christoph Heyne of Lancaster. Early forms that are rare in American pewter are also great finds, even when they are not marked.

Britannia ware is not esteemed so highly as the old pewter. This is not because of the quality of the metal, but because of the design and craftsmanship of the objects made in it. Since this alloy was popularized at about the time when spinning was introduced, it was fashioned by the new, more mechanical process. At the same time a general shift in taste was introducing heavier designs and greater elaboration.

Britannia ware offers plenty of variety, however, and often pleasing design and sound workmanship if you look for them. Most familiar names in that period are the Danforths and the Boardmans of Connecticut, who shipped pewter all over the country; and the English makers, James Dixon & Co., and Townsend & Compton, both of whom must have exported tremendous quantities of pewter and britannia to America, to judge from the amount that is still here.

There are two schools of thought about the care of old pewter. Some people prefer to keep it dull, some like it shined. There's no law about it, and you can take your choice; but after all, it was originally bright, and early owners undoubtedly kept it looking as much like silver as possible. If you do shine it, be careful to use a soft metal polish, no abrasives. And never put it on the stove.

7. Tinware

Before the days of mail-order catalogues, even before the country general store with its assorted stock of everything from yard goods to pickles, it was the tin peddler who supplied many household needs of the farmer's wife. Early in the spring he set out in his loaded wagon from the manufacturing towns of the East and toured the countryside through New England, Pennsylvania, New York State, along the Ohio Valley, and even as far down the Mississippi as New Orleans.

The Yankee peddler was the great disseminator of the Connecticut shelf clock, the Hitchcock chair, New England cotton goods, pewterware, buttons, and many other products of the early industrial era that eased the life of families in outlying regions and on the frontier. After 1830, especially, until almost the time of the Civil War, he did the work of the railroads and the steamboats which finally put him out of business. He also took the place of the party-line telephone, spreading news and gossip. He operated on a barter basis, receiving local produce in exchange for his varied goods.

The itinerant peddler's great stock in trade, the one that gave him his name, was tinware—pots, pans, and ovens, dippers, cups, and plates, candle molds, pudding molds, cookie cutters, lamps, candlesticks. By 1830 the American tinsmith, or whitesmith as he was also called, was providing a great variety of useful wares at low cost.

Many of these are still to be found today, often rusted and battered in testimony of the hard uses they served. Some are painted with gay designs, which may now be faded and peeling. More are unpainted, and though less colorful they too are often decorative.

Since tin is soft, it was easily ornamented with punch-work, piercing, or crimping. Sconces and other lighting fixtures often have crimped or scalloped edges. Coffeepots frequently have punchwork in ornamental designs. Piercing was effective in the panels of pie cupboards. Children's alphabet plates have the letters stamped around the edge and a picture in the middle.

Alphabet Plate

The great majority of these things were made after the Revolution. In contrast with pewter, which is composed chiefly of tin, tinware is composed chiefly of iron. It is, in fact, thin sheet iron coated with tin. Since there is no natural tin in the United States, and since England preferred to send manufactured products rather than raw materials to her Colonies, little tin was available here in colonial days. From the 1790's on it became steadily more plentiful and a sizable tinware industry grew up, whose leading center was in Berlin, Connecticut.

The most appealing of the old tin is the painted ware. Often called *japanned ware,* it also goes by the French name *toleware,* though *tôle* really refers to all tinware, painted or not.

Japanning is one of the many arts the Occident learned from the Orient. It was an attempt to imitate Oriental lacquer.

Painted Mug

In China and Japan, the making of lacquer has been a highly developed art for centuries. Lacquer is made from lac, a gum extracted from a certain tree and carefully prepared, with artificial coloring. It is painstakingly built up in successive layers and polished. Then its hard shiny surface is decorated in various ways, often in relief. When the English became acquainted with this Oriental lacquer in the 1600's they called it japan, just as they called porcelain china.

In trying to achieve the effect of this lustrous, colorful surface, Europeans used colored varnishes as a substitute for the true lacquer. On furniture they built up relief designs with a composition called *gesso,* and covered them with these varnishes, which were then polished. Often they added gilding and silvering. On tinware they used the varnish without trying to achieve relief decoration, and added a baking process to fix the glossy finish.

While it originally suggested a hard shiny finish, japanned ware eventually came to mean any metalware with painted decoration. Pewter as well as tin was treated in this way in Europe.

The original English center for this product was at the village of Pontypool in Monmouthshire near Wales. This was an iron-manufacturing town in the 1600's, and experiments with japanning began there before 1700. In time quite an industry grew up which spread to the neighboring village of Usk, and also to Birmingham, Bilston, and Wolverhampton.

Painted domestic utensils of all sorts were produced, especially from about 1760 to 1820. Typically the background was black, crimson, brown, or mottled like tortoiseshell. The decoration of flowers, exotic birds, scenes, and festoons was delicately painted and touched with gold or silver, which gave it an effect of richness.

Similar work was done on the Continent, especially in France, where bright red or green backgrounds with designs in gilt became more typical. Both there and in England it remained a fashion until well into the 1800's, though after 1820 japanning began to be done more on the lightweight papier-mâché than upon tin, as before.

Lace-Edge Tray, 1800

In America the beginnings of painted tinware came after the Revolution, when the tin itself became more plentiful, though some japanning on furniture had been done many years earlier. The real popularity of painted tin extended through the first half of the 1800's.

The earliest painted wares are trays, and the earliest type made in America is the round *lace-edge*. It was painted black with small colored flowers in the center or forming a wreath within the perforated edge. Examples, made shortly before and after 1800, are rare.

A still earlier type that was made in England, but apparently not in this country, is called the *Chippendale* tray. It dates from the Chippendale period, mid-1700's to our Revolution, and has a wide scrolled

Chippendale Tray, 1760's

rim rather like the scrolled edges of silver trays and tables of the same time. It is usually oblong, larger than the lace-edge, and its decoration is in keeping with its rococo shape. Characteristic designs are garlands, peacocks, and fountains in colors, finely painted against a black or green ground.

By the 1820's and 1830's the tray form had become simplified and was a plain rectangle with oblique or oval corners and a shaped "hand hole" at either end. Painted de-

Octagonal Tray, 1820

signs became larger in scale and typically consisted of floral motifs spreading out from the center. Backgrounds were dark and the designs were in naturalistic colors. Scenes, probably copied from prints, were also produced. At this time the stenciling

Oblong Tray, 1830

process was adopted for tin decoration and continued side by side with freehand painting for many years.

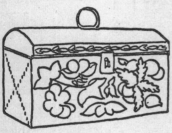

Painted Box

The technique of tin painting has recently been revived and is now practiced by many women who enjoy restoring the worn designs on old tinware. There are two basic types of work for this kind of decoration which are done in the traditional manner: freehand painting with brushes and oil colors, and stenciling.

Stenciling requires the use of cutout paper stencils to shape the units of a design, which are applied in colors or bronze powders or both. The colors are painted with a brush. Bronze powders—which is the old name for metallic powders in tones of gold, silver, and colors—are rubbed on. Similar techniques were used for decorating Hitchcock chairs and some other furniture, as well as walls and floors in many homes.

Besides trays, the forms most often found in old painted tinware are teapots, coffeepots, tea caddies or canisters, baskets, bread trays, and boxes for many a purpose,

Bread Tray

from two-inch trinket boxes to capacious lunch boxes. Bright red, yellow, green and blue are the usual colors of the designs, contrasting with a background of brown-black or red.

Coffeepot

Probably some of these things were decorated at home, but tin painting was a recognized craft at which many people made their living, particularly in New England and Pennsylvania. In general New England designs are somewhat more restrained than those of Pennsylvania, but both are delightfully gay and colorful.

8. Iron, Brass, and Copper

Many of the basic necessities of colonial life were made of iron. Nails, hinges, and latches were essential for the very houses people lived in, and iron tools and implements of all sorts for both indoor and outdoor use were equally indispensable.

Early records list such numerous and varied articles as hoes, saws, axes, hammers, chains, plowshares, pitchforks, kettles, skillets, spits, gridirons, jacks, shovels, tongs, andirons, fenders, trammels, pot hooks, grates, locks, steelyards. Some of these necessities were made of brass and copper as well as iron.

These things are fun to collect today, particularly if you have an old house to put them in. There are collectors who specialize in tools used in agriculture, building, or various crafts. Some of them are now obsolete and identifying their uses offers tantalizing puzzles.

Aside from tools, latches, and hinges, the most numerous of these old metal articles are equipment for the fireplace and the devices for lighting. These are both discussed in separate chapters.

Ironwork

Essential though iron was in colonial days, it was not nearly so plentiful as it is now. Much ironwork, and at first bar iron itself, had to be brought from England. The first successful iron foundry in America was established in 1644 at Saugus, Massachusetts, where the Old Ironmaster's House still stands and is open to the public. Soon foundries and forges sprang up all over the Colonies, converting the native bog iron into usable form.

The ironworker here was generally the village blacksmith, who did everything from shoeing horses to making andirons or mending locks. In England the craft was divided between the blacksmith, who made the cruder implements, and the whitesmith, who did the finer work with iron and steel.

Up to the time of the Revolution, and even for a generation afterward, most of the finer iron goods used here came from abroad. Fine locks and tools were chiefly English. Even such things as firebacks and the familiar H and HL hinges were imported, though some were made here.

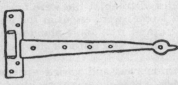

Under the circumstances, it is often difficult to tell the source of the old ironwork we find, or even the approximate date. Rarely do pieces have any sort of identifying mark. Latches and hinges sometimes have an impressed date; utensils sometimes have a date or initial or even the name and location of the maker; but these are exceptions to the rule.

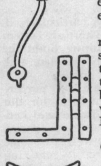

The kind of things made in iron did not reflect the trends of style that affected sophisticated furnishings, and the same types continued to be made for generations. Iron trivets, pans, toasters, and broilers used in Ohio in the 1830's are virtually the same as objects used in New England a full century earlier.

Cast Iron

Wrought-Iron Hinges

By 1840 cast iron had virtually replaced wrought iron. Iron casting had not been unknown before that. It had been done in Europe since the 1300's, and in America by all the early ironworks. It was the process by which firebacks were made, and many of the andirons, pots, kettles, and other utensils of daily use. But as practiced it was essentially a hand craft, just as was the blacksmith's process of working iron with forge and tools to make what we call wrought iron.

In the 1800's it became an industry, and cast-iron

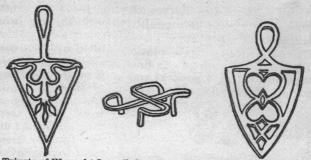

Trivets of Wrought Iron (left and center) and Cast Iron (right)

products became essential in other lines of industrial development. New methods of refining and manufacturing iron introduced it to many new uses.

Cast iron became an architectural material, for one thing. Cast-iron railings, balconies, fences, mantelpieces became the vogue. They are still to be seen on nineteenth-century houses all over the country, particularly in the South where New Orleans and Mobile are justly proud of their "iron lace." Cast-iron deer appeared on the lawns, and hitching posts in the form of jockeys, black boys, horse's heads.

Furniture was cast in iron. Nowadays nineteenth-century iron benches are enjoyed as garden furniture, but in the 1850's cast iron belonged in the parlor and bedroom too, in the form of marble-topped tables, chairs, and bedsteads. Cast-iron stoves were everywhere, some of them fancy to the point of being fantastic, reflecting the current tastes for neo-gothic, neo-classic or just novelty.

Cast iron made possible many innovations and embellishments of household equipment, such as sewing

Sadirons

machines, washing machines, apple parers. The old-fashioned "smoothing irons" were replaced by cast, heavy flatirons called sadirons, or by hollow ones that could be filled with hot coals.

Cast iron also provided a quantity of smaller useful and decorative objects, from toothpick holders to mirror frames. Lamp bases were frequently of cast iron. Cast-iron bootjacks, used today as door stops, are often amusing in form. The cast-iron penny banks that encouraged thrift in the young are now enjoyed by their elders too. These small objects date for the most part from the 1860's to the 1880's.

Cast-Iron Bootjack

Brass and Copper

The early history of brass and copper making in America is as obscure as that of iron. There were workers in these metals here in the 1700's, but few of them are known by name. We know that Paul Revere manufactured copper, besides being a silversmith and engraver and famous horseman, and we know of several other early coppersmiths and braziers from their advertisements and from rare marks on their work. The coppersmiths worked in brass as well, and often in pewter and tin.

Copper is the chief ingredient of brass, and mining and refining copper presented difficult problems before the metal could be worked at all. Toward the end of the 1700's copper sheets were produced here, by hammering and later by rolling, and they were also imported.

American metalsmiths of the late 1700's and early 1800's advertised kettles of all sizes, saucepans, tea kettles, chocolate pots, coffeepots, and stills, of both brass and copper. One finds such things today, and also warming pans or bedwarmers, pitchers and measures, mortars and pestles, chafing dishes, andirons and fire irons. The copper pudding molds that people like to collect today are chiefly of the second half of the 1800's, or later.

About the most varied, decorative, and still useful early brass wares are candlesticks. In the 1700's they served as a less expensive substitute for silver, and their forms followed approximately the same changes in style as those in silver. The earlier, heavier examples are extremely handsome but rare today.

Up to about 1670 brass candlesticks were cast in a solid piece. From then until about 1790 a method of casting them in two pieces and soldering or brazing the hollow halves together was used. You can usually see the seams on these, which give a clue to their date. After 1790 again, solid casting was resumed, but you can tell late examples from the earlier by differences in style.

Furniture hardware, which is referred to in the chapter on *Furniture,* represents another important group of early brasswork. Clock dials were made of brass up to about 1770; the numerals and usually some decoration were engraved. Small ornaments called *appliques,* applied to clock dials and other parts of furniture, were cast in brass.

In the early 1800's brass castings were much used on furniture in the neo-classic styles, for feet and for applied decorations in such forms as acanthus leaves, rosettes, lion masks. These small ornaments are called *ormolu,* from the French words for ground gold, though they were not actually gilded in most cases, nor did the alloy of which they were made contain gold. Some were polished and finished by hand after being cast and are fine and delicate in workmanship.

By far the greater part of the brass and copper used here in the early days is of European make, and a great deal that is on the market today has been recently imported. Much of it is from Holland, which has always been prolific in brasswork, and some is from France. At the town of Dinant in Belgium brassworking reached such a peak in the 1400's that *dinanderie* came to be a common name for domestic utensils of brass. England too has produced much fine brassware. And the American craftsmen worked in the European tradition. There seem to be no simple and sure rules for telling the product of one country from another.

Weathervanes

One thing made in iron or copper that we can usually identify as American is the weathervane. Not that the use of weathervanes is an exclusively American custom: they have probably been used wherever the wind blows. Early European ones of wrought iron are often very decorative.

But the familiar American ones have certain typical forms that seem to be our own—the cock, of course, in many guises; the Indian; the horse; such regional forms as the fish, the whale, the ship, the long-horn steer; agricultural emblems like the plow and farm animals; and many fanciful, topical, or symbolic devices such as the mermaid, the racing trotter, the angel Gabriel blowing his horn. The variety and amusing ingenuity of our weathervanes is extraordinary, and their design and workmanship are often so good that they are now ranked as American folk art.

The simplest weathervanes are silhouettes cut out of a flat plank of wood. Less often examples in wood are carved and whittled in low relief. Those of metal are likewise either flat or modeled in the round. The flat ones were cut out of sheet iron, occasionally with two or several pieces bolted or riveted together.

Wood and iron weathervanes are usually painted, as much for protection from the elements as for decoration. There are weathervanes that have been swinging over churches in the East since the 1700's, but few have survived exposure to the weather for over a hundred years.

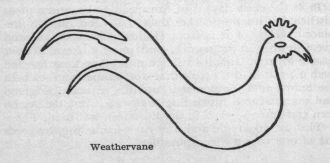

Weathervane

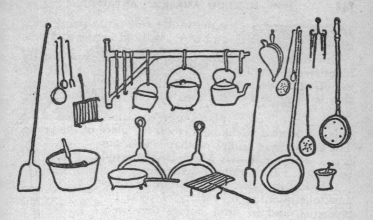

9. Fireplace Equipment

Around and within an old open fireplace there used to be quite an assortment of pots, skillets, ladles, skewers, and other utensils made of brass, copper, and iron. These were the standard cooking equipment in American homes throughout colonial days and well into the nineteenth century, for cooking stoves did not even exist before the 1830's and did not come into really general use, particularly in the country, until after 1850. Before that, cooking was done over the open fire. Remarkably good and varied cooking it was too, done by roasting, baking, broiling, and all the processes that we now achieve with our electric gadgets and pressure cookers.

In the earliest houses in America one room served as kitchen, dining room, and living room too, and its fireplace opening was immense, eight or nine feet long and five feet high. As bigger houses were built and greater ease of living developed, the rooms took on more specialized uses, and the kitchen became a separate room. In the South it was customarily even a separate building, and many of the small detached kitchens are still to be seen there.

The essential equipment of a cooking fireplace was the strong iron *crane* which was fixed to the brick or

Iron Kettle

stone inside and could swing back and forth, to hold kettles and pots over the flame; *kettles* and *pots* themselves; utensils for stirring, spearing, and mixing; *andirons* or *firedogs* for supporting the fire; *fire irons* for tending it. In earliest fireplaces a green sapling called a *lug pole,* suspended in the back, took the place of the crane. The kettles were hung by S-shaped iron *pot hooks,* or by *trammels* whose length could be adjusted by a ratchet arrangement.

Practical purposes did not require a tremendous quantity or variety of these implements, and in most homes they were fewer and simpler than the accumulations with which some collectors like to clutter their fireplaces today.

Baking was done in the hollow oven built in the brick or stone within or beside the recess of the fireplace. Such an oven, incidentally, is properly called a *brick oven* —or stone, as the case may be—and not a Dutch oven. The name *Dutch oven* belongs to a covered iron pot, or, as frequently used today, to a three-sided tin box-shaped object which was placed on the hearth and used as a reflector oven. The long-handled tool like a flat shovel, used for taking hot things out of the oven, was called a *peel.*

Roasting was done on a *spit,* in its simplest form an iron rod stuck through a piece of meat and suspended over the fire. Sometimes the spit was rested on hooks on the andirons, sometimes it had an iron standard of its own. Sometimes a rather elaborate device called a *clock jack* was used. This had an attachment with gears and pulleys which could be wound up, and as it unwound kept the spit slowly revolving at an even

Iron Peel

Iron Trammel

rate. Small spits for quail or other fowl sometimes had a tin reflector behind, and a pan for the juice.

Besides the basic essentials, fireplace equipment included such other metal objects as toasters, gridirons, trivets on which to rest hot dishes, pipe tongs, plate warmers, wafer irons. A *footstove* sat on the hearth and a *bedwarmer* was leaned nearby, ready to be filled with hot coals. A pair of *bellows* was kept handy to fan the coals to flames. Purely functional as they are, these things are often highly decorative.

For kitchen fireplaces, andirons and fire-tending tools were ordinarily of iron, utilitarian and simple in design. Sometimes an extra pair of low andirons was used to hold the back log in place. Sometimes the upright part of the higher andirons had hooks for holding a spit at various levels. Simple shovels and tongs sufficed for tending the fire.

In less prosperous houses andirons were not used at all. The fire had to be kept burning continuously and built up a fine bed of ashes, and a couple of stones or old bricks would do to support the logs.

Wrought-Iron Toaster

Bellows

Footstove

Wrought-Iron Broiler

Jamb
Hook

In the 1700's houses became larger and grander, and the number of fireplaces multiplied. There had to be one in every room, for they were the only source of heat. People discovered that smaller, shallower fireplaces threw out greater heat.

In the living, dining, and bedrooms, fireplaces became an ornament as well as a necessity, and were framed in paneling or decorative woodwork which covered the chimneybreast, to the ceiling. This whole frame was the *mantelpiece*, or *chimneypiece;* the decorative treatment above the opening was the *overmantel*. The protruding *mantel shelf* to which the name mantel is now given did not appear until nearly 1800.

With such fireplaces, more ornamental andirons were used, made of brass, or less often copper, in combination with iron, and fenders were placed in front of the hearth. Fenders were supposed to keep sparks from flying out into the room, but many of them were too low to be very practical and were chiefly decorative. Fire tools—shovel, tongs, and poker—were made with brass handles to match the andirons, and brass *jamb hooks* were fastened to the wood fireplace frame to hold them.

You will find very few brass andirons today made much before the Revolution—that is, andirons with the entire upright part and the legs of brass. The shank or horizontal part was always iron. More usual were those made all of iron, or with just the tip or finial of brass.

Besides the simple wrought-iron ones, there are some later andirons with the upright part cast in the shape of a Hessian soldier, or sometimes of George Washington. These are of the 1800's.

By the later 1700's the classic taste in decoration affected andiron design like

Andirons of Wrought Iron,
early 1700's

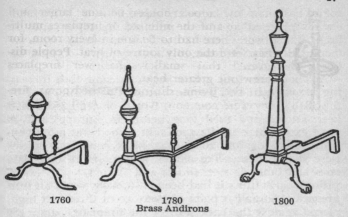

| 1760 | 1780 | 1800 |

Brass Andirons

everything else, and the very attractive type appeared which is frequently reproduced today. It has a brass column as the upright member, square-sided and tapering, or baluster-shaped, tipped with an urn-shaped finial.

Fenders of about the same period are usually of wire, not in a mesh, but arranged vertically between brass

Brass, 1810

or iron bands at top and bottom. Such fenders range in height from about 12 to 24 inches; the lower ones are older.

Heavier, lower, and more ornamental fenders all of brass or of steel had been used earlier in Europe and in some of our more elegant houses. Some eighteenth-century French ones in brass, for instance, are composed of ornate leaf forms. The more usual type in England in the 1700's was shaped from a flat sheet of metal and pierced and engraved in decorative designs. The earlier ones were a single straight strip; later they were serpentine or bowed.

By the early 1800's when the Empire style was apparent in furniture, it brought a new form to andirons and fenders. Andirons, still of brass, became heavier and rounder, often with a large

Cast Iron, 1850

round ball on a low baluster-shaped column. Wire fenders disappeared and were replaced by lower ones in brass. These were either curved sheets pierced in ornamental designs, or fence-like arrangements of bars between low posts.

At about this time grates began to come into increasing use, as coal became more readily available, and by the 1840's they were common. Grates or fire baskets had been known and used long before in Europe, and to some extent here in the 1700's, but wood was more generally used for fuel than coal. Most commonly grates were simple basket-like affairs of iron; more elaborate ones had brass or steel finials and facings.

From early times it had been customary to use an iron *fireback*—a large flat plate of iron two or three feet high, placed against the back wall of the fireplace, partly for ornament and partly to protect the brick or stone. American firebacks often have arched tops and are cast in patriotic, armorial, religious, or conventional designs in low relief—George Washington on horseback, the arms of England, Abraham and Isaac, floral motifs. These continued in use until well into the 1800's.

As the nineteenth century advanced the fireplace lost its place of honor in the home to heating stoves. The Franklin stove had been invented before the Revolution and by the end of the century had come into fairly general use. It was essentially a fireplace of metal, moved out into the room so the heat could radiate further. It seemed a great improvement over the old-fashioned fireplace, and soon was improved on still further. By the 1830's cast-iron stoves made by modern methods had become available and from then on grew so popular that many a family walled up its fireplaces and fitted stovepipes into the chimney.

Where fireplaces persisted, they became more and more ornamental. Carved marble or elaborate cast-iron mantels were the thing. The opening was small, often arched, and a grate was usual instead of andirons. Fenders of cast iron were made in neo-gothic and rococo designs that were in keeping with the furniture in the room.

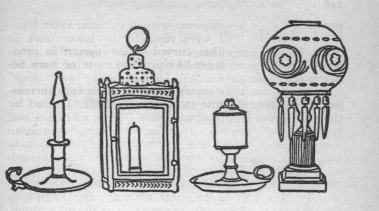

10. Lighting

The dark ages of the world continued right up to our own time. That is hard to remember in these days when bright lights are a commonplace and candlelight is romantic. It is not so long, however, since candles were a luxury, and the best light most people had was the even feebler glow from a tiny lamp.

The first real improvements in illumination were made late in the 1700's, and for another whole century after that there was still very little light in most people's lives. The forms of lighting used in colonial America were just as primitive as those of Biblical days, and in fact very much the same.

Though candles may seem more archaic to us than lamps, both lamps and candles go so far back into antiquity that we cannot trace their beginnings. Indeed, the lamps worked on the same simple principle as candles—that a bit of fabric soaked in grease of some kind will burn slowly and give off a little light. The only variations in the universal primitive type were in the kind of grease and in the shape of the container, which was the lamp. Local types were developed, of course, depending on available grease for fuel and available materials for the lamps, but they are all related fundamentally.

Earliest American Lamps

The average early home in America got most of its light after sundown from the open fire. To eke out there would be the small and odorous flame of a *betty* or *phoebe lamp,* and possibly a candle or two, but candles were neither cheap nor plentiful. They had to be dipped or molded of tallow (animal fat), or of wax from bees or berries. More readily available was the *rushlight,* which was just a piece of rush from a nearby swamp, soaked in grease and ignited.

Betty Lamp

Phoebe lamp is the American name for a universal primitive type called in England the *crusie.* It is simply a small open cup or dish to hold the oil, widened at one point into a groove or channel for the wick. Sometimes a second dish is attached below to catch any oil that may drip.

Often the phoebe lamp is called a betty lamp, but strictly speaking the betty lamp differs from it in having a little built-in narrow slot to support the wick, instead of the plain groove. It may or may not have a cover. Both phoebes and betties usually have hooks attached to hang them by. Both types were used here from the days of the first settlers.

Related primitive types also used in America are the *pan* lamp and the *spout* lamp. The former, with a floating wick in an open pan, was apparently brought from Germany and is found most in Pennsylvania. The spout lamp has a cylindrical channel or spout for the wick instead of an open channel like the betty. In some regions the local kind of spout lamp was called a *slut* lamp.

These small and relatively ineffective early lamps were all made of iron or, less often, tin or pewter. Pennsylvania pan lamps were also sometimes of pottery. For wicks people ordinarily used old rags or twisted cotton threads. For fuel they used animal fats or vegetable oils or fish oil—and one smelled as bad as another. Whale oil came into use in the 1700's, but it was costly and hard to get in America until after the War of 1812, when our own whaling industry was greatly increased.

The rushlight, which served in country and frontier regions well into the 1800's, was put in a wrought-iron *rushlight holder*. This was a clamp on a standard. Some old devices combine a candlestick and rushlight holder.

Candlesticks

The simpler candlesticks used in America were of iron, tin, pewter, or pottery, but brass, silver, Sheffield plate, porcelain, and enamel provided the equipment for more elegant homes. Up to about 1800 candlesticks were usually much more ornamental than lamps, for candles were the more fashionable kind of light.

Most if not all candlesticks used in America were of the *socket* type, with a socket to hold the base of the candle. The *pricket* type, with which the candle is impaled on a sharp spike, is apparently older, but both were used in Europe by the 1300's, and by the time America was settled the socket type had become more common.

1650   1720   1750   1760   1790
Candlesticks

Not many of either type were used here before 1700, to judge from the few to be seen today. There are rare examples in brass with spreading or domed bases, and still rarer ones in silver. These were almost all made abroad. The majority of the sticks from 1700 on are also imported, and there are probably many more of them in this country today than there were in the eighteenth century.

These candlesticks are tremendously varied, and follow the styles of other antiques. There are the baluster-stem forms of the early 1700's, related to Queen Anne silver forms; the rococo of the mid-century; and the neo-classic of the late 1700's and early 1800's. The main trends are shown in the sequence of forms illustrated.

These were made in silver and, as a less expensive substitute, in brass. Pewter was also less expensive, but less frequent than brass. From about 1750 on, handsome sticks were made in Sheffield plate, and in enamel. Glass ones are fairly rare before the late 1700's.

Early sticks sometimes had a slot in the socket through which something sharp could be poked to pry out the candle stub. Eventually brass and tin sticks were made with a lever in the shaft to achieve the same end. Some candlesticks had a *grease pan* or *drip pan* encircling the stem, midway, just above the base, or near the socket. In others the spreading base served the purpose. Silver and Sheffield plate sticks after about 1760 often have an inner, removable socket, with a wide flange or rim called a *bobèche*.

There were in the 1700's what appear to be miniature candlesticks, which are called *tapersticks*. They were used for small tapers instead of full-size candles, and were made in silver, brass, and glass.

Short candlesticks with a handle, intended to be carried about and to light you to your chamber, are called *chambersticks*. The early "frying-pan" type has a flat rimmed pan for a base and a wide, flat handle. More commonly seen are those made after 1750 which have a molded saucer base and a ring or scroll handle.

For carrying a light outdoors there are many kinds of *lanterns,* whose walls must both shield the flame and let out light. One of the most familiar types is cylindrical, with pointed top, made of tin and

Tin Lantern
1820-1850

pierced in a decorative design to let the
light through. This is commonly miscalled a "Paul Revere lantern"; actually
it was not developed until long after the
patriot's famous ride and was made chiefly between 1820 and 1850. The lanterns
that were hung in the steeple of the Old
North Church for Paul Revere that night
were tall, rectangular, with metal frame,
glass panes, and a round, pierced, double
cap on top to aid ventilation. One of
those very lanterns is still preserved in
the Concord Antiquarian Society.

Lantern,
late 1700's

Hexagonal or octagonal lanterns of a
similar type were also used in Revolu-
tionary times. Early lanterns were often rather crude,
homemade affairs, with frame of wood and panes of horn
instead of glass.

Since candles and lamps provided inadequate illumination at best, people made the most of every means of

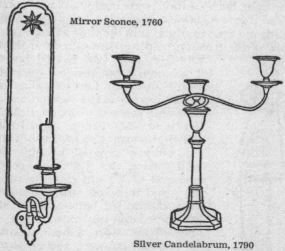

Mirror Sconce, 1760

Silver Candelabrum, 1790

intensifying what light they gave. In the eighteenth century there was a widespread preoccupation with light,
and all sorts of reflectors were devised. Mirrors had a very

real purpose. Candle fixtures for the wall, or *sconces,* often had a small mirror or a polished plaque of silver or brass behind the candle, or in humbler types a shiny piece of tin. Candle brackets were often attached to the frames of large mirrors, both the flat rectangular ones of the 1700's and the round convex type of about 1800.

Lights were multiplied by the use of *candelabra,* branched sticks for holding two or more candles; and *chandeliers,* hanging fixtures for many candles. The period of cut glass in the late 1700's and early 1800's contributed its considerable share to the cause of lighting. Candlesticks with faceted stems reflected the light even better than shining silver or brass, and it could be further intensified by prisms hung from thin bobèches. Candelabra were made of glass, and also of silver, brass, and the other materials used for candlesticks, particularly Sheffield plate.

Chandeliers were the most brilliant of all, made all of metal, wood, or glass, or of glass combined with metal, often with festoons and shafts of cut-glass prisms to intensify the light. Such creations were made at Waterford during Ireland's great glassmaking period, and also in France, England, and even in America in the early 1800's. Around the turn of the century the prisms are usually small, and round or oval, like faceted buttons. The long, straight-sided ones date after about 1820. Less imposing chandeliers were made of pewter, and for American country churches a chandelier sometimes had a turned wood center and arms and sockets of tin.

A simpler type of hanging light used during the eighteenth century consisted of a plain clear-glass bowl, deep oval in shape, with a brass candle socket in the bottom, and a shallow domed disk suspended above it by brass chains. More elaborate lanterns for indoor use were rectangular or hexagonal, and had clear glass panes set in an ornamental brass frame. Incidentally, the familiar kind with col-

Glass Hanging
Lantern, 1700's

Toleware Candelabrum, 1820

ored and etched glass in its sides is not colonial, but dates after 1850.

All these devices, however, did not dispel the gloom of the eighteenth-century interior, for the only sources of artificial light remained the candle and the primitive lamp. At last in 1784 a Swiss physicist named Aimé Argand invented a new kind of lamp, and soon one improvement in illumination followed another. Still it took time for the new inventions and discoveries to be given practical application, and much more time for the results to reach the average home.

Through the first quarter of the century at least, and even up to 1850, candlesticks were used in greater quantity and variety than before. Candles became less costly, with more plentiful tallow from whale blubber, and more practical with the plaited wick which was invented about 1820. Candlesticks of silver, Sheffield plate, brass, and pewter continued in popularity, and between 1825 and 1840 a good many were put out in britannia metal. Ceramic candlesticks of the 1700's and 1800's represent most kinds of porcelain and pottery, from Meissen to Bennington, from English creamware to Pennsylvania redware. Tin, painted and unpainted, wrought iron, and cast iron all contributed their share.

Following the delicate faceted glass sticks of the period shortly before and after 1800, pressed-glass candlesticks were made in some quantity, including the hexagonal baluster and dolphin forms that people like to collect

Cast-Iron
Candlestick, 1840

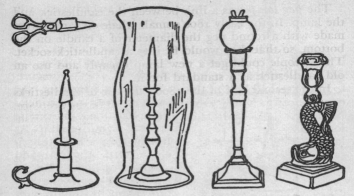

Left to Right: Chamberstick with Extinguisher and Snuffers,
Hurricane Shade, Candlestick of 1800 with Peg Lamp,
Pressed-Glass Dolphin Candlestick (1850)

today. Bohemian glass produced tall, prism-hung candle-sticks in sets of two or more which were used as mantel garnitures in the 1850's. They usually have wide saucer tops and their red, green, or yellow glass is ornamented with gilding and engraving.

These are generally called *girandoles,* though that name really refers to a branched candle holder. It is some-times applied also to candle brackets on a mirror frame, and often to the round gilt-framed convex mirrors of about 1800, even when they have no candle brackets.

Necessary accoutrements of candles were *extinguishers* and *snuffers*—which were not the same thing, but for quite opposite purposes. An extinguisher was to put the flame out, and looks like a dunce cap. Snuffers were for clipping off the burnt wick to make the candle burn more evenly and brightly. Of silver or brass, they look like scissors with a little box attached to one blade, and were usually equipped with an upright stand or flat tray.

The tall glass cylinders called *hurricane shades,* within which candlesticks were set to protect the flame from breezes, seem to have been used particularly in the South and in the West Indies. The earliest ones date from the late 1700's and they continued in use up to the mid-dle of the 1800's. The later ones are often engraved.

The *peg lamp* was a link between the candlestick and the lamp. In the early 1800's small whale-oil lamps were made with a round peg the diameter of a candle on the bottom, so that they would fit into a candlestick socket. Thus people could get a new lamp cheaply and use an old candlestick as a standard for it.

In the second half of the 1800's the use of candlesticks experienced a change something like that of the fireplace. No longer a necessity, candles were considered old-fashioned and were partially eclipsed by the splendid new lamps and gas lights. But nothing can take the place of candlelight, any more than of an open fire, and the use of candles and decorative candlesticks has not ceased.

Lamps of the 1800's

Though improved lamps did not immediately replace candles after Argand's invention, they became gradually more efficient and more numerous.

Small whale-oil lamps with closed font and upright burner holding one or two small wicks were the first to replace the betty lamp. They had appeared before 1800, though they were not common in this country before 1820. Benjamin Franklin is credited with having invented the double-wick idea, to double the light shed by a single lamp. In these lamps the two short metal tubes for the wicks were originally stuck through a cork fitted in the neck of the reservoir, but presently a metal collar took the place of the cork. The burners are often missing from the examples of such lamps which are to be found today.

Pewter Lamps, 1820-1840
Left and center, for whale oil; right, for camphene

The whale-oil or sperm-oil lamps are extraordinarily varied in size, shape, and material. Most of those to be found in pewter, britannia metal, and tin date from the 1820's through the 1840's. They may be fairly tall with a shaped stem below the font; or low, with or without a handle, sometimes with a saucer base. They were eventually superseded by the more ornamental glass lamps.

Solar Lamp, 1850

When camphene came in as an illuminant in 1830, it was used in the same kind of lamps as whale oil, but a different kind of burner was devised. This difference was necessary because camphene, a mixture of turpentine and alcohol, was not only inflammable, but explosive, and it was important to take precautions. While the wick tubes for whale oil barely top the collar through which they are inserted, those in camphene burners project a couple of inches, and when there are two they slant apart from each other. They usually have little metal caps hung on chains to extinguish the flame and keep the fluid from evaporating.

Both camphene and whale oil continued in use until about 1860 when they gave place to kerosene. Though the lamp chimney to increase the draft had been invented before 1800, open-flame lamps were the general thing until about 1860.

Oil Lamp, 1860

Meanwhile many more imposing and ornamental lamps were being put on the market, incorporating the principle of Argand's invention. This consisted essentially of a tubular or cylindrical wick in a round burner, which permitted air to reach the wick from both inside and out. Its importance lay in the fact that with its increased draft this hollow wick gave a much brighter flame than had ever been achieved with the flat or solid wicks

Brass Kerosene
Lamp, 1880

previously used. Argand's invention was far-reaching in its effects and had many applications and adaptations in lamps of this central-wick type.

One of the most popular was the *astral* lamp with its variants, which had the burner supported on a projecting arm so that it was lower than the fuel reservoir. Astral lamps were often extremely ornamental, made in Sheffield plate, brass, cast iron, Wedgwood jasper, or other china, and bedecked with hanging prisms. They came in sets of two or three, to stand on a mantel, and had small globular or oval glass shades. They were put on the market about 1820 but their period of greatest popularity in America was the 1850's. Their fuel was whale oil.

Another of the ornamental adaptations of Argand's principle popular in the 1850's was the *solar* lamp. Its font or fuel reservoir was under the burner and stood on a metal or marble column hung with prisms; a large glass globe, engraved or etched, was used as a shade.

Lamps for whale oil had been made in blown glass and blown-three-mold before the day of pressed glass, but probably not many. Examples are small and low, sometimes with handle and saucer base. A few, called *wineglass* lamps, are blown or pattern-molded.

In the lacy-glass period of the 1840's, taller and more elaborate lamps were made with blown font and lacy base. Eventually other parts of the lamp came to be pressed, and the lacy designs were replaced by bolder patterns. Pressed-glass lamps continued to be made into the kerosene era after 1860, and on up to the 1900's. The colorful faceted overlay lamps were chiefly a product of the 1850's and 1860's.

Decorative painted porcelain and

Student Lamp, 1880

earthenware lamps competed with glass lamps for popularity, and the two materials were combined in lamps. Both were likewise combined with brass or cast-iron mounts and marble bases. Entire lamps were also made of these metals, and of silver, Sheffield, bronze, and the painted tin called toleware.

Parlor Lamp, 1890

Throughout the 1800's there were constant developments in the mechanics of lamps as well as in their shapes and decorative features. To present-day taste these changes did not always improve the appearance. One type of the kerosene period that has had a recent revival is the brass *student* lamp which was much used from 1875 until after 1900. With its reservoir supported higher than the burner, it is somewhat related to the earlier whale-oil astral lamp. Perhaps that is why it was called a "colonial" lamp in its time, though it was no more colonial than it is "antique" today.

Of about the same late period are the *parlor* lamps in glass or china, composed of a large bulbous or globular base and matching shade, flamboyantly painted with flowers. These are now known as "Gone with the Wind" lamps because they were shown in the moving picture of that name and shortly enjoyed a tremendous new popularity. Actually they date not from Civil War times but from the 1880's and 1890's.

Development of Lighting

A few of the milestones in the development of modern lighting are helpful to keep in mind as guides to dating and understanding old lighting equipment:

1784—invention of the Argand lamp and the lamp chimney

1792—first use of artificial gas for illumination

1815 and later—growth of the American whaling industry, increasing availability of whale oil for lamp fuel and tallow for candles

1820—first production of plaited wick, used in candles and lamps

1830—development of camphene as a lamp fuel

1859—discovery of petroleum, providing kerosene as a lamp fuel

1880—invention of the electric light

These dates are all merely points of departure. For instance, though gas light was used in England before 1800, it was a novelty at Castle Garden in New York in 1825. And while astral lamps and gasoliers illuminated fine mansions, many an American home was still using betty lamps like those of the Pilgrims, even after 1850.

Old Lamps for Modern Use

One of the most difficult problems for people who want to use antiques suitably and sympathetically today is what to do about lighting. It's simple enough to use antique chairs, antique china and glassware, but who cares to smell up the house with an antique betty lamp, or try to read by candlelight, or run the fire hazard of a kerosene lamp? A few collectors who have re-created eighteenth-century interiors very completely do use candles, or one-candle-power bulbs in early candle holders that have been wired for electricity, but even they have concealed electric lights that can be brought out for practical purposes.

There are many antiques that can be converted into lamps, and not merely things that were lighting devices originally. Of the latter, many of the nineteenth-century whale-oil and kerosene lamps can perfectly well be electrified. Candlesticks and candelabra may make attractive lamps, but it would be too bad to convert any item that had real antiquarian value.

The most generally satisfactory bases for lamps are old vases and bowls in china, or in glass or metal. These are of manifold sizes, shapes, colors, and textures and often make handsome, well-proportioned lamps.

In converting a piece it is important to remember that the shade becomes part of the electric lamp and must be considered in relation to the base. A vase or early lamp that is charming in itself may look ridiculous when you put a shade of the necessary size and shape on top of it.

It is even more important to remember that this business of making something into a lamp can go too far. There has been a mania in the past few years for "making it into a lamp," and some quite deplorable conversions have been perpetrated. Dolls, tin toys, pottery dogs, coffee grinders, even Kentucky rifles have been wired, and then further distorted by shades in fancy shapes trimmed with large pink bows.

There is no law against making an old coffee grinder into a lamp, of course; what is against it is its incongruity. A lamp is first of all a light, second a decoration. To fulfill its second function, it should be not only pleasing in form, material, and decorative detail, but also appropriate to the setting in which it is used. The coffee grinder may be appropriate in the kitchen, but it does not belong in the living room.

As a test of whether to convert a given object into a lamp, set it where you expect to use it, and decide whether you would enjoy keeping it there as an ornament, not as a lamp. If you wouldn't, don't think that electrifying it will make you like it any better.

11. *Coverlets and Rugs*

Homespun and handwoven would describe the great majority of fabrics used in colonial America. Brocades and velvets, satins and damasks were not unknown, of course, but they had to be imported and they were costly. Most of the materials for people's clothes and for the curtains and upholsteries, bed and table linens of their households, were far less elaborate. They were made of native wool and flax and, later, cotton. Spinning and weaving were done in almost every home, though there were also professional weavers here from the early 1700's on.

About the time of the Revolution the first steps toward mass production of textiles were being taken in England with new inventions for mechanical spinning and power-driven looms. In 1791 Samuel Slater set up the first spinning mill in America at Pawtucket, Rhode Island, appropriating the principles introduced by Richard Arkwright and jealously guarded in England.

Not many years later power looms were established here to convert the new thread into cloth. By the 1820's the Jacquard loom, a French invention, was also adopted here, making possible a much greater variety and complexity of woven patterns. Fabrics of all sorts became more available, more varied, and less expensive.

As with so many industrial developments, however, the

old hand methods did not immediately become obsolete, and the spinning wheel and hand loom continued in active service in many a home until nearly 1850. In some regions, indeed, they have been used much more recently.

Textiles are among the most perishable of our antiques, and relatively few survive from colonial days. There are more from the 1800's, and among the most interesting are bedcovers and rugs. Bedcovers of various kinds were made by industrious American housewives—embroidered, stenciled, and a type called wool-on-wool which is related to the hooked rug—but those most familiar today are the woven and the quilted.

Woven Coverlets

The old handwoven coverlets are of two main types, *overshot* and *double-woven*. Both are of wool, with linen or cotton for the warp or vertical threads. In the overshot type the pattern is formed by long threads that "skip" or overshoot the foundation. This is the kind woven by women on their own home looms, of yarn they had spun on their own spinning wheels, from early colonial days on. It is the kind of weaving that is usually done today by women who practice the old handcraft.

Double-woven coverlets are actually double, with the pattern appearing in reverse on the under side. These were usually made by professional weavers who traveled about with their looms, stopping at a home long enough to weave the yarn on hand and then moving on. They date between about 1725 and 1825.

Another, and rarer, type of coverlet which also had a reverse pattern is called *summer and winter* weave. It was made chiefly in Pennsylvania, and examples are a good deal rarer than of the other types.

The yarns for these early coverlets were home-dyed

with vegetable dyes and the colors are most often blue and white, though red or brown was also used with white, or white alone. Synthetic or aniline dyes did not become available until 1856. Since the looms were narrow, coverlets had to be woven in strips and sewn together; they always have a seam down the middle.

The fine, geometric designs in which these coverlets were woven are extraordinarily varied. They were passed on from one generation to the next, and spread from one part of the country to another. Their traditional names are perhaps less descriptive than imaginative—such delightful names as *blazing star, cat track, chariot wheels, walls of Jericho, lover's knot.*

The introduction of the Jacquard loom in this country made possible a new type of woven coverlet, with pictorial designs. These were made by professional weavers and frequently have names of people and places and dates woven into the corners.

The name of the weaver was often given, and sometimes that of the owner too. They were made in many parts of the country, and examples dated from the 1830's to the 1860's indicate how long coverlets of this type were popular. Often a motto or fine sentiment was also woven into the corner, such as *Agriculture and manufactures are the foundation of our independence.*

These Jacquard coverlets occur in both single and double weave, and usually in a single breadth without a seam down the middle. The designs are chiefly naturalistic, with large roses and garlands, eagles and patriotic emblems, peacocks or other exotic birds, animals, buildings, trees. A favorite border design is *Boston town* which portrays prim houses among Chinese pagodas and palm trees. Another, at the head of this chapter, pictures Inde-

Double-Woven Coverlet

Overshot-Weave Coverlet

pendence Hall with eagles and Masonic emblems. Green was add to the colors used earlier and frequently occurs in combination with red and white.

Quilted Coverlets

Quilts are another colorful kind of bedcover, into whose making our great-grandmothers put many hours and countless stitches. The patchwork variety is the most familiar, and it includes two kinds, *pieced* and *appliqué*. In the pieced quilts, the small pieces of which the design is composed are sewn together along their edges. In ap-

pliqué quilts, small pieces are "laid on" or applied to the foundation and fastened with invisible stitches around their edges to make up the design.

Quilts of both types have been made since early days, but, due to time and hard use, few have endured from the 1700's. Most of those that are found are from the 1820's to 1860's and there are later ones.

The patterns of patchwork quilts are infinitely varied, and have descriptive or symbolic names like the woven coverlets. *Star of Bethlehem, log cabin, rose of Sharon, princess feather, Whig rose, wheel of fortune,* are only a few of the more familiar. Geometric patterns seem to have been more popular in New England, while Pennsylvania liked florid, naturalistic ones in brilliant colors, but quilt patterns spread all over the country and are known by different names in different regions. A universal type was the *crazy quilt,*

Patchwork Quilt Patterns

which had no set pattern but used up left-over swatches and snippets of every size and shape.

In fact, the earliest quilts were probably crazy quilts, made of remnants of worn-out wool and linen garments. Later, printed cottons of various kinds were used. By the mid-1800's, when quilts were made as much for show as for warmth, crazy quilts and others were made of bits of silk and velvet, sometimes painted, and trimmed with featherstitching.

In the 1840's and 1850's *autographed* quilts were the vogue. Also called *album* or *friendship* quilts, these were made for presentation. Each block was sewn and signed by a different friend of the recipient, who was generally a bride.

Then there are the *all-white* quilts, the rarest of all. Some people consider them also the handsomest, especially those with exquisitely quilted all-over designs.

Occasionally they were stuffed or corded to make the design

Patchwork Quilt Patterns

stand out in relief. More common are the *candlewick* spreads, which are not quilted with a needle but have a relief design in heavy cotton yarn or candlewick, either woven in on the loom or worked in by hand. Plaited candlewick such as we know today was not invented until the 1820's and most candlewick spreads date after that. In older coverlets of this kind the candlewick formed loops or ridges; after the 1840's it was clipped so that the design appeared tufted.

Tufted candlewick spreads have been made by hand

in the southern mountains right up to the present time, and they have also, of course, been made by machine for years. A machine-made descendant of the early type, ridged but not tufted, is the so-called *Marseilles* coverlet. It is a Jacquard weave with the design in low relief, and became popular in the late 1800's.

Hooked Rugs

No one needs to be told what a hooked rug is. Examples are common in homes, in department stores, along roadsides where they are hung up for sale. They are simulated in broadloom carpeting and linoleum. Many women enjoy making them by the old technique of hooking wools or thin strips of cloth through a burlap or coarse canvas foundation. But familiar as they are, most people know little about them. Hooked rugs are widely believed to have been the typical floor covering in colonial American houses.

Actually, no one knows the origin of the hooked rug, but we do know that the type was not made here as early as colonial days. Probably it originated in French Canada and came down over the border into New England, where more hooked rugs were made than anywhere else in this country.

It is unlikely that any examples were made here before 1800, and certainly the great majority were a good deal later. Those that exist today are mostly less than a hundred years old. They are still made—in greater quantities, no doubt, than ever before—and they are used more extensively now than they ever were in their true "period," which reached its peak in the 1860's and 1870's.

In early colonial days, that is up to 1725 at least, floor coverings were sparse. In most homes the floor remained bare, or was sprinkled with sand. Sometimes a bearskin or other animal hide with the fur still on it was thrown on the floor.

By the 1700's, "Oriental" rugs were brought from the Near East, but they were not for everyone in those days, any more than they are today. They were used as table covers more often than as floor coverings. While they came into increasing use as carpets for homes that could

"Rising Sun" Quilt

afford them, many floors remained bare. Some were covered with heavy canvas "floor cloths" that were varnished or painted with ornamental designs, and others with homewoven or embroidered rugs.

Before 1800 fine French carpets from the Aubusson and Savonnerie factories were being imported, but they, like Orientals, were in the luxury class. Carpet manufacture in imitation of Brussels carpets had begun in Great Britain in the mid-1700's, and Axminster, Wilton, and the "ingrain" carpeting from Scotland were known here before the end of the century.

Not till the 1830's, however, did machine-made carpets become plentiful enough to be popular. From then on they were widely used, but many homes, particularly in the country, still depended on home industry for their floor coverings, and that is where the hooked rug, the braided rug, and the rag carpet come in.

All three of them were ways of getting more wear out of worn-out garments. Faded fabrics were dyed to give them new life, and torn into thin strips. To make rag carpets they were woven on the home loom, as yarn would be, with a heavy cotton or linen warp. Braided rugs, round or oval, were made simply by plaiting rag strips into a long braid, coiling it up, and sewing it fast. Hooked rugs offered the greatest scope for creative expression.

The most numerous hooked rug designs are floral. There are all kinds of flowers and all kinds of designs, some charmingly composed, richly colored, and finely worked, some naive, coarse, or crude. Animals, birds, patriotic emblems, geometric motifs, scrolls, and garlands are other frequent designs.

Perhaps more interesting though not always so successful are the original designs which the rug-hookers made up or copied from the scenes about them—a house, a farmyard, a ship. Some of their designs they copied or adapted from prints, no doubt, or from fabrics, wallpapers, or more elegant rugs. Stamped patterns were available if a woman lacked inspiration for her rug design, and these were probably responsible for many of the more conventional designs.

A type sometimes confused with the hooked rug is the *shirred* rug. It was made by sewing thin strips of cloth, which were shirred or gathered, to the surface of the backing instead of hooking them through it. The general appearance is rather like that of a hooked rug, and the designs, usually floral, are similar. Old shirred rugs are a good deal less common than hooked, and apparently no one has the patience to make them today.

12. Pictures

The chances are that when someone says "antiques" to you, one of the first things you think of is Currier & Ives prints. These prints belong with the Boston rocker and the Staffordshire teapot and the steeple clock and the hooked rug and all those other trimmings of the average nineteenth-century American home which are old enough to seem quaint but young enough to seem familiar. The important thing about them is not their age, nor their artistic quality, but their subject matter.

Harry T. Peters, the great collector of Curriers who wrote the monumental book about them, called Currier & Ives "printmakers to the American people." They were to their day what *Life* magazine and the newsreels are to ours. They provided the latest news in pictures of everything that was going on from sport to war, and the pin-up girls, the comics, the portraits of great men living and dead, plus a vast lot of pretty pictures of every conceivable subject, suitable for framing.

Nathaniel Currier started in business in New York in 1834. In 1857 he took James Merritt Ives into partnership with him. Currier retired in 1880, and Ives a few years later. Then for some time the firm was carried on by the sons of the two partners, but it was petering out and finally was closed out completely in 1907.

The prints they made are lithographs, printed from stone (calcareous slate). Lithography was a new process when Currier started in business. Invented in Bavaria about 1795, it had spread to France, England, and the United States before 1820. Soon it flourished because it had the advantages of so many inventions of the time: it offered a cheaper and quicker way of making pictures in quantity than had been known.

Up to about 1880 the Currier lithographs were printed in black, and then colored by hand with water colors. In the 1880's and later, they were generally printed in color from a series of stones. The firm employed many different artists to draw the pictures, of whom the best known are Fanny Palmer, Louis Maurer, George Henry Durrie, Thomas Worth, and Arthur F. Tait.

The prints vary greatly in size. Some are only about as big as a postcard. The commonest are what are called small folio, measuring about 9 by 13 inches. Most highly prized today are the large folios, about 18 by 27 inches in size.

The American people provided a ready market for pictures, and Currier & Ives provided prints for every taste. There are over seven thousand subjects. Mr. Peters classified them under the following headings:

Views, chiefly American; political cartoons and banners; portraits of notables; historical events; certificates; moral and religious subjects; sentimental portraits and scenes; pictures for children; country and pioneer home scenes; humor; sheet music covers; Mississippi River views; railroad subjects; emancipation; financial speculation; horse prints; hunting and fishing; sporting events —prize fighting, racing, baseball, and so forth; current events—fires, disasters, and the like. No aspect of contemporary life was omitted.

The prints vary in quality as well as in subject. Some of them deserve to be considered as works of art but most of them do not. Their greatest value today is as a pictorial record of one of the most active and vital half-centuries of our country's history.

The subjects most highly prized by collectors now are the winter scenes, Mississippi River views, sporting, ship, horse, and railroad prints. *Home to Thanksgiving* is a perennial favorite. Views of towns, cities, and specific locations are increasingly popular and valuable. Recently the so-called sentimentals—pictures of pretty girls, or of the sailor and his lass—have been finding new favor.

Currier & Ives Print, "Home to Thanksgiving"

While Currier & Ives were in business they sold their small prints for six cents apiece wholesale, colored or uncolored. The most expensive of the large ones went for three dollars apiece retail. Today there is a difference. You can occasionally pick up a small one, especially if uncolored, for a few dollars, but the more desirable ones go up into the hundreds, and a few over a thousand.

Condition of course affects the value of a print. Prints that are stained can sometimes be cleaned but it is safer to entrust the job to an experienced print dealer than to try it yourself. Many of the Currier & Ives prints have been reproduced, and some of the reproductions are very hard to tell from the originals.

Other American Lithographs

Currier & Ives were the leading American lithographers of their day but they were certainly not the only ones. Prints by hundreds of other firms exist, and some of them are finer in quality than the Curriers. Worth knowing about are the prints of Kellogg of Hartford, Pendleton of Boston, Endicott of New York, Huddy & Duval of Philadelphia, Sarony, Major & Knapp of New York, Bufford of Boston and New York, and numerous others.

Chromolithographs

About the time of the Civil War, American lithographers began using the lithographic process for printing in color—actually printing several colors from a series of stones, one for each color, instead of painting them by hand on a single-color print. These color prints, as distinguished from colored prints, are called chromolithographs. Though most lithographers adopted the process, the nickname "chromo" is associated with cheap sentimental and commercial pictures turned out in the late years of the 1800's, which have no artistic or historic interest and so are not sought after by collectors.

Other Prints

Lithography is only one kind of printmaking. Aquatint, mezzotint, etching, stipple, and line engraving on copper, wood engraving, steel engraving, are all processes that you should investigate if you are seriously interested in prints, but they belong in a more specialized book than this.

Of particular interest to most of us are the views of cities, towns, and scenic wonders in America, and there are a good many since the subjects were of great interest in the 1800's too. Then they were novelties; now they make striking comparison with the way the same places look today. Probably the finest American views, artistically speaking, and also the rarest, are those in aquatint.

More familiar are the small hand-colored engravings after drawings by the English artist, William Henry Bartlett. A hundred of these subjects were published in the 1830's and 1840's as illustrations for a book called *American Scenery*. They were frequently copied by American lithographers and painters, and also by designers of the Staffordshire printed earthenware of the period. They were, in fact, the source of a considerable number of the historical views that were produced on the "old blue" china to appeal to the American market.

Among other attractive small prints are the colored fashion plates published in *Godey's Lady's Book* and other magazines in the second half of the 1800's. Nowadays these engravings, which are incidentally a good guide to the history of nineteenth-century costume, are often taken from the volumes and framed as separate pictures. So are many small colored flower and bird prints issued as illustrations for botanical and ornithological books in the same period of the 1800's.

Universally known and admired are the Audubon bird prints. John James Audubon (*1780-1851*) was an American naturalist who classified and portrayed the birds all over North America. The prints from his water-color drawings were originally published in Great Britain between 1827 and 1838, issued in parts which were bound in four volumes called *Birds of America*. This is the famous Elephant Folio edition, which measures 39½ by 29½ inches. There are 435 aquatint plates, colored by hand. The first ten were engraved by William H. Lizars; the rest were by Robert Havell and Robert Havell, Jr., who also retouched Lizars' plates.

These plates are highly prized today for their decorative quality and their excellence as examples of printmaking, not to mention their ornithological importance. The great favorite is the *Turkey Cock*—the American wild turkey, not the barnyard fowl—which was Number One of the series. Incidentally, the complete *Birds of America* was originally sold at $1,000; it has recently brought over $15,000 at auction.

In 1860 a new issue of the *Birds of America,* in the same large size but in one volume, was put out in New York. Only 106 plates were included, and they are chromolithographs by J. Bien. In 1840-1844 a miniature edition had been published by Audubon in New York and Philadelphia, and reissued in 1856, 1861, 1865, and 1871. It comprised seven volumes in octavo size, with 500 plates lithographed by J. T. Bowen.

Less well known than the Audubon birds are his pictures of animals, the *Quadrupeds of North America*. These were published by J. T. Bowen, in both folio and octavo size. The printmaking process by which they were produced was lithography.

There are, of course, bird prints by other artists and printmakers, such as Mark Catesby and Alexander Wilson earlier and the Englishman John Gould later. These also have great merit and interest, but Audubon is generally considered to be the master in this field.

American Primitive Paintings

Relatively few people in nineteenth-century America could afford to own fine paintings by leading artists, but they did have other pictures than prints on their walls. There is a certain type of painting which must have hung in many homes, and includes portraits, still lifes, pictures of places and events, scenes of daily life, memorial pieces. Though they vary in quality as in subject, they have these characteristics in common: they are highly stylized, have a flat, linear quality, and show a distorted perspective. These pictures are now known as American primitives or folk art. The best of them have vigor and vitality, simplicity, and directness. The worst of them are just plain crude.

Most numerous of these pictures are the family portraits. There are paintings of stiff matrons in wide lace collars, or forbidding gentlemen in high white stocks, of children with toys, of family groups. These were usually done by itinerant artists who traveled about the countryside and painted wherever they could get an order. Most of such pictures are of the 1830's through the 1860's, though there are some both earlier and later.

Besides the itinerants there were numerous others who made their living by painting in oil or water color at that time but who never will be ranked among the great masters. Many of them painted carriages and signs as well as pictures, and their pictures reflect their craft technique. Some had no training in painting of any kind, although a few studied under academic painters.

To many people today, the interest of these non-academic American paintings is not so much esthetic as historic. Like Currier & Ives prints, they make a pictorial record of nineteenth-century America—an informal, personal record, told by the people themselves. The best of them, however, are admired as works of art, and examples hang in museums and private collections. Edward Hicks, William Matthew Prior, Thomas Chambers, Eunice Pinney, Erastus Salisbury Field, Joseph Whiting Stock, are a few of the painters whose works are especially appreciated and are recognizable by their style.

Pennsylvania Fractur

The Germans who settled in Pennsylvania brought with them from Europe the custom of having an elaborately lettered and decorated certificate of birth or baptism and framing it to hang on the wall. These certificates, called *Taufscheine*, were written in German and illuminated with hearts, flowers, angels, birds, and various other symbolic or decorative motifs, painted in water

Pennsylvania Baptismal Certificate

color with charming naiveté. They are called *fractur schriften,* from the German name for an early kind of type or script, a name which came originally from the Latin *fractura* and referred to the "broken" letters of Gothic calligraphy.

Up to the late 1700's fractur work was done by hand and sometimes it shows as fine lettering, embellished initials, and well-composed designs as medieval illuminated manuscripts, from which, of course, it is descended. Later, certificates were printed, with blanks for filling in names and dates, and the pictorial decoration was painted by hand.

Besides the certificates for vital statistics, fractur work includes various other kinds of pictures related to them in technique and design. Some of these were done, like the *Taufscheine,* by schoolteachers or professional scribes; some were amateur work. There are, for instance, portraits of national heroes, pictures of Adam and Eve, still-life compositions, and conventionalized designs in the typical Pennsylvania motifs. Their colorful designs are quite fascinating in their variety.

Miniatures

It was a charming custom in the 1700's to have one's miniature painted to give to someone near and dear. In those days before photography, it provided the only portable portrait. The custom goes back much further in Europe, but in America it was at its height in the late 1700's and early 1800's. Miniatures were painted on ivory, usually oval, two or three inches high, and mounted in a gold frame or locket, or in a velvet case. Some of them are exquisitely done and can be truly appreciated only with a magnifying glass.

These were painted by skilled artists, of whom the leading ones in America were Edward Greene Malbone, Benjamin Trott, Charles Fraser, James Peale and other members of the Peale family, John Ramage, Archibald and Alexander Robertson. There are miniatures of George Washington, Lafayette, and many another illustrious personage in museum collections. There are also

Silhouettes

many of unidentified subjects by unidentified painters which remain hidden away among family heirlooms. Perhaps you are lucky enough to have a miniature of one of your own ancestors, possibly signed by the artist.

Silhouettes

An inexpensive version of the miniature was the silhouette, which was particularly popular here in the first half of the 1800's. A silhouette could be painted, but usually the name refers to a cutout profile portrait.

The commonest type was hollow-cut: the head was cut away, leaving the white paper frame silhouetting a hole. This was then mounted against a black or dark background of paper, cloth, or painted glass.

The other type was cut from black paper and it was the head or figure that was preserved rather than the frame around it. This was then pasted to a light background, which might be painted or lithographed to provide an appropriate setting.

Sometimes whole groups were mounted together. Bust portraits are the most common, but full-length figures are not unusual. Occasionally the silhouette was touched up with ink, water color, or gilding.

In this country many an amateur tried his or her hand at silhouette cutting but there were a number who made a business of it. Silhouettes by one of the "names" are desirable, but plenty of the anonymous ones are

Silhouette
by Brown

interesting portraits well worth having.
William King, William Bache, William
Doyle, Charles Willson Peale, are among
the best-known of the professionals who
made hollow-cut bust portraits. Master
James Hubard, who came from Great
Britain and worked in Boston, Philadelphia, and Richmond, made full-length
and bust portraits of the cut and pasted
type. Augustin Edouart, a Frenchman,
traveled all over this country in the 1840's
cutting full-length portraits which he usually mounted against sepia backgrounds.
One frequently sees entire family groups
by Edouart, cut and mounted in this way.

William Henry Brown, a native of
Charleston, is known for his silhouettes
of *Distinguished American Citizens,* from Henry Clay to
Daniel Webster. The 27 full-length portraits, black
against an indoor or outdoor setting, were reproduced
by lithography in a book published by Kellogg in 1845.
This book was reprinted in facsimile in 1931, and when
the silhouettes have been removed from the binding,
as they often are, it is difficult to tell an original from
a reprint.

There are numerous other cutouts in addition to silhouette profiles—flowers, eagles, conventionalized designs—and some of them are unbelievably intricate. Besides being framed as pictures, such things were used as
valentines and other sentimental missives, and sometimes
also they were carefully mounted in albums.

Daguerreotypes, Ambrotypes, and Tintypes

The invention of photography by the Frenchman
Louis Daguerre in 1839 introduced new kinds of pictures
that were soon to supplant miniature portraits and silhouettes. To most of us, all those small faded metallic
portraits in little black cases are daguerreotypes, but
actually these early photographs are of three different
kinds. *Daguerreotypes* are on silver; *ambrotypes* are on

glass; *tintypes,* which came along later, are on iron coated with collodion. True daguerreotypy was already becoming obsolete by the mid-1850's and was rapidly replaced by new improvements which led to modern photography.

Most of these early pictures are family portraits, and don't interest you much unless they happen to be of your own family. Those that show scenes or events, however, are likely to be important historically, and well worth preserving.

Daguerreotype cases are often found in antique shops today. Sometimes the pictures have been torn out and thrown away, and the velvet-lined cases converted into cigarette boxes. These cases are occasionally of real or imitation leather, but the majority are made of an early plastic which was cast in molds. The ornamental designs impressed on them include scenes and historical events, as well as conventional motifs characteristic of the period, and sometimes they are very finely executed. The most elegant cases have insets of mother-of-pearl.

Samplers

Women have always made decorations for their homes, and among their creations have been pictures of various kinds, though not all were originally made to hang on the wall. In the 1700's when a little girl was taught to sew she made a sampler, with rows of all the plain and fancy stitches she had learned. The earliest samplers were long and narrow, and were really exemplars of the child's prowess with the needle.

Later samplers became more pictorial and less varied in stitchery, being worked chiefly in cross stitch. They

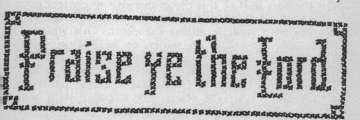

showed houses or trees, animals, birds, or flowers, all in a conventional arrangement framed in decorative borders, with a verse or pious sentiment and the worker's name and age. By the early 1800's samplers became less fine in workmanship and design, and after the 1830's or so the custom of making them died out.

Needlework Pictures

More elaborate needlework pictures had been made in the 1700's—pastoral scenes copied from engravings, or coats of arms, or floral compositions—worked in needlepoint which completely covered the canvas. By 1800 this type had gone out of style. Embroidered pictures were worked in silks on a satin ground, and such details as faces and hands were often painted in oil instead of being worked with the needle. The compositions were usually floral, sentimental, or mourning subjects. Such pictures were made up to the 1830's.

Before 1850 a new kind of needlework picture had become popular, called *Berlin woolwork* because the patterns, wools, and canvas came from Germany. It was done chiefly in needlepoint or cross stitch with heavy wools of brilliant, often garish colors. In technique it was rather like the eighteenth-century needlework pictures, but was much less fine in design, color, and workmanship. Designs were often historical subjects or copies of famous paintings. Sentimental pictures of flowers, birds, and animals were also great favorites.

Household Arts

In the first half of the 1800's one of the genteel occupations which "young gentlewomen" were taught was painting with stencils, called *theorems*. This was done either in water colors on paper, or in oils on velvet. With the aid of the stencils various designs could be composed. The most usual were still-life groups—a bowl of flowers or a basket of fruit. Such theorem paintings, as they are called, are often very effective with their stylized compositions and shaded colors.

Young ladies also did a good deal of freehand painting and much of their work is now classed among American primitives. Romantic views, copied from engravings or drawing books, were popular, as were memorial pieces with a symbolic weeping willow beside a tomb.

Godey's Lady's Book and other publications of the 1800's were full of instructions for making ornamental bits of handiwork, and plenty of examples survive to prove that women followed them. There are the shell-work wreaths and bouquets, hung in deep mahogany frames or set under a large glass bell, which date chiefly from the 1840's to 1870's. Making artificial flowers, working mottoes and bookmarks, doing beadwork, preserving leaves and grasses, drawing in pastel on sandpaper, painting on china, are only a few of the other household arts which have left us decorative souvenirs.

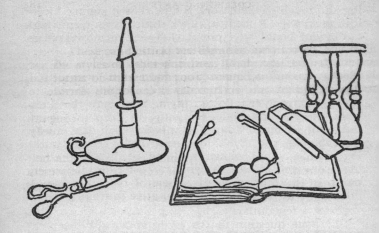

13. Collecting Antiques

The great majority of our antiques are the home furnishings of the past—the furniture, china, glass, and other things discussed in this little book. There are also, however, many other sorts of venerable objects that people enjoy collecting. These often appeal as much for sentimental as for artistic reasons.

There are, for instance, the old dolls and toys which were loved by children of bygone generations. Antique playthings include tiny china tea sets, doll-house furniture, and a variety of other miniatures that are irresistible to many grown-ups today.

There are firearms, more essential to the early settler than a roof over his head, and the powder horns that he used with them. There is the carved whalebone called scrimshaw that sailors made to while away the long hours of their three-year whaling voyages. There are carved butter molds, chalkware figures, cigar-store Indians, buttons, fans, shawls.

It is impossible even to list all the antiques people enjoy collecting, still less to do them justice. A whole book, for example, could be written about old boxes. It would include the paper hatboxes of the 1830's, the colorful Pennsylvania bride's boxes, the neat little wooden boxes made by the Shakers. And it could not overlook the elegant little eighteenth-century snuffboxes of enamel, gold, or silver, or the later ones of papier-mâché, or the engraved brass tobacco boxes from Holland and Germany. There are carved Bible boxes of Pilgrim days, urn-shaped mahogany knifeboxes that stood on Hepplewhite sideboards, slant-topped pine saltboxes that gave their name to the early slope-roofed New England houses.

All these things and many more are among the heirlooms from the past that delight collectors of the present. Some of them command prices well up in the thousands, but many worth-while and interesting antiques are to be had for a few dollars each.

The one question that is asked about antiques more than any other is the most difficult to answer: what are they worth? There is no set scale of prices for antiques. The exquisite artistry of some, the historical significance of others, is impossible to measure in dollars and cents, and what is one man's trash is another man's treasure.

The law of supply and demand has a great deal to do with prices of antiques. If hundreds of collectors are all looking for the same kind of thing, prices are bound to go up, because the supply is limited and fixed. A pressed-glass tumbler, for instance, may bring more than a blown-glass goblet that is a good hundred years older. There are fads and fashions in collecting, but the astute collector is the one who does not follow the crowd.

A Currier & Ives print once brought $3000 at an auction, just because two people there happened to want it very much and bid each other up. The same print has frequently sold for a fraction of that amount.

Geography also affects values in antiques. Prices for similar things vary in different parts of the country, because of local tastes and interests. In general, American antiques command higher prices in this country than comparable objects made elsewhere. Each country prizes the things that are part of its own background.

You may find a Sheraton chair in one of the leading shops priced at five times what you paid for a very similar chair at a country auction. When you buy from a reliable dealer, however, you are paying not only for the antique but for the benefit of his knowledge, experience, and judgment.

If you wish to get a specific appraisal, the best thing to do is to consult an experienced appraiser, antique dealer, or auction gallery in your locality, and pay a fee for the information. Dealers and auctioneers are also the ones to turn to if you have antiques you wish to dispose of. They know the market—it is their business to know.

Everyone has heard tales of the unsuspected treasure

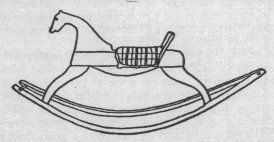

—a little table picked up for a song that turned out to be a genuine Duncan Phyfe, or an old chest found in a chicken coop and sold for hundreds of dollars. It has happened, and it may happen again, for there are still heirlooms hidden away in attics and barns whose value is unsuspected by their owners. If you have old things, find out what they are and what they are worth. This applies to old papers and books and pictures as well as furniture.

Do not assume, however, that just because things are old they have fantastic value. It often happens the other way too. You should not be insulted if a dealer offers you less than a fortune for your grandmother's old plate.

Many things that we cherish because of their personal associations would have no great value to anyone else. In many cases, the satisfaction of owning family pieces cannot be compensated for by the dollars and cents they would bring if offered for sale. Really, the value of an antique is what it is worth to you.

Some of your heirlooms may have no financial worth in the current market, but still have historical value and be well worth preserving. When you are clearing out the attic, consult your local historical society and museum as to whether they would like anything you have to dispose of.

These institutions will also be helpful in identifying your antiques—those you want to keep. They usually make it a policy not to give appraisals, but they will give information as to the date, source, and historical interest of antique objects in many cases.

To find the answers to such questions takes knowledge and experience, but you can learn to find them yourself. Many of them, as well as much useful related material, have been published in the specialized magazines and books. There are hundreds of helpful books on the subject that go into far more detail than this one. You will find that the more you learn about antiques, the more there is to learn, and books are one of the best sources of information about them.

Books that identify makers' marks on old china, silver, and pewter are mentioned in the preceding chapters. A few other marks are helpful guides in dating certain things that are not very old but are frequently seen among antiques.

In 1891 the United States government passed a tariff law requiring goods imported to this country to show the country of origin. Therefore anything marked *Made in England* (or any other country), or just marked with the name of the country, is later than 1891.

From 1842 to 1883 the British Patent Office used a diamond-shaped mark on goods that were registered, or patented. Certain letters and numbers in the corners of the diamond are code symbols that indicate the date the design was registered. Thus pieces so marked may be later than that date, but they are not likely to be earlier. Since 1883 British registered goods have been marked just *Rd.* with a number.

The mark *Déposé*, which occurs on French goods after

the mid-1800's, is the French equivalent of the British *Registered* and the American *Patented*.

The best way to learn about antiques, to develop your own taste and judgment, is to study antiques themselves. Look at them and train your eye to observe fine points of style, decoration, material, and construction. Handle them and learn the feel of old things. Visit museums, shops, and the homes of your friends who have antiques.

There have been collectors as long as there have been people. Collecting American antiques was a fad a hundred years ago. Now it is more than a fad. All over the country people are finding enjoyment and satisfaction, not only in collecting antiques but in living with them. These things were made to be lived with. They have been used in the homes of America for three hundred years, and they are bringing charm, individuality, and a sense of permanence into American homes today.

Index